T0150616

THE
STRONG
MIND

IRH PRESS

BOOKS
IRH PRESS
New York

Library of Congress Cataloging-in-Publication Data

ISBN 13: 978-1-942125-36-5
ISBN 10: 1-942125-36-4

Printed in Canada

First Edition

Cover Design: Whitney Cookman
Interior Design: Juicebox Designs

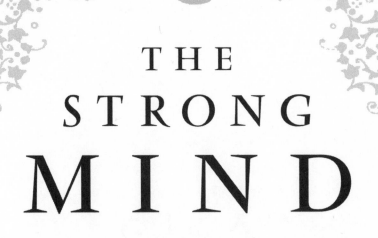

THE
STRONG
MIND

The Art of Building the Inner Strength
to Overcome Life's Difficulties

RYUHO
OKAWA

IRH PRESS

●

TABLE OF
CONTENTS

●

3

CULTIVATING INNER MATURITY

4

DEVELOPING INNER RICHNESS

5

THE POWER OF THE STRONG MIND

PREFACE

In this book, *The Strong Mind*, I present essential ideas that epitomize my thinking on the mental attitudes we should cultivate and my philosophy on life during the period when I was maturing as a religious leader. These pages show the ways to overcome life's obstacles and barriers, the human qualities that will enable you to achieve great success, and vital secrets to triumphing in your life.

What I went through during the last several decades after my spiritual awakening strengthened my heart and mind and helped me develop my capacity and depth as a person. In this period, I tasted suffering and sadness to a degree never experienced by an average person.

Over the years, I have produced a vast body of published works and lectures that include a diverse array of perspectives, and all of them represent the days I spent cultivating a strong mind through hardship.

Each day, whether it brought raging wind, rain, or swelter, I sought to transform the weak mind into a strong mind. And as I have walked the path to self-improvement, my other self has always been there, watching over my every step on this journey.

Ryuho Okawa
Founder and CEO
Happy Science Group

BUILDING
RESILIENCE AGAINST
LIFE
CRISES

CHAPTER

1

LIFE CRISES ARRIVE ONCE EVERY DECADE

1

The Underlying Message of the Proverb "Fall Seven Times but Rise Eight Times"

I would like to begin this chapter with a discussion of a common Japanese proverb, "Fall seven times but rise eight times," which describes a mind that never gives up. Actually, I've always thought that this count was a bit odd. If you fall seven times, you can only get up seven times. So I've been wondering for some time how it would be possible to fall seven times but rise eight times. But I figured that the key here is probably that we need to be determined to rise one extra time every time we fall. Put another way, if bad things happen to us seven times, we should do eight good things so that we can bring about a positive outcome in the end. I believe that this is the point of this saying. Although the numbers don't technically add up, the saying conveys the importance of adopting a spirit of resilience; we must be ready to rise to our feet one extra time as we face life's trials and tribulations.

I find it quite interesting that the numbers used in this proverb, *seven* and *eight*, seem to match the average number of major crises that we encounter during our several decades of living in this world. This may be a nugget of wisdom that has survived in the form of a proverb to help us weather the vicissitudes of a lifetime. Through the course of our lives, we face an average of about seven critical situations that can become stumbling blocks, so we should be prepared to rise up eight times to end our lives on the positive side. This means that we encounter a major life crossroad about every ten years.

●

CHILDHOOD:
A Period of Crisis within the Family

The first period in which we encounter a crisis is usually around age ten, or in fifth or sixth grade. This often involves family trouble: a quarrel, divorce, or layoff. It could also be a school-related problem such as a conflict with a friend, bullying, or truancy. These are the issues we most often encounter in our childhood.

TWENTIES:
A Period When We Suffer Our First Major Setbacks of Adulthood

The second major crisis usually arrives at around age twenty, give or take a few years. Everyone gets tested before reaching adulthood. This test may involve choosing an academic or career path. It is also during this period that we struggle to begin serious relationships or find life partners. And this often triggers our first disappointments as adults that have a life-changing impact on us. This is a common experience that we go through in our late teens or early twenties.

THIRTIES:
A Period When Our Ability to Provide for Ourselves and Our Families Is Tested

We usually become fully financially independent around age thirty. This is a period when our ability to be truly self-reliant is tested. We may face the financial challenge of becoming self-sustaining without relying on others' support. If we are married, we may face concerns about our ability to provide for a family. In any case, something will happen to measure our competence as full-fledged, independent adults in our late twenties or early thirties.

●

FORTIES:
A Period When We Face Difficult
Work Issues or Health Problems

There are two basic kinds of challenges we are likely to face as we approach forty. By this time, many of us have achieved mid-level managerial positions. We face issues related to job promotion, which is often a benchmark for our further career advancement to top executive positions. But statistically speaking, more than half of employees unfortunately never make it past mid-level managerial positions during their lifetimes. This percentage may vary depending on the occupation or industry, but it is more or less the same in each field. In trading firms and other commercial enterprises that have a large number of managers, about half of the employees can reach middle-management positions. But in manufacturing companies with large workforces, only about 10 to 15 percent of employees can achieve managerial positions. This is an example of a possible barrier to success that we may face in our work lives.

We may also face crises relating to health or family. If you are raising a family while working full-time, you may find it increasingly difficult to recover from fatigue as you approach forty. The busyness of everyday life may start taking a toll on your body and cause health problems. Your condition may often be exacerbated by family troubles that involve your children, since children's troubles tend to become more serious and frequent as they age.

Age forty often marks a turning point for our bodies; we begin experiencing many symptoms and health problems that we didn't experience in our younger days. Hormone changes occur during this period, and many women start going through menopause between their late forties and early fifties. At first, many of them do not realize that they are experiencing menopause symptoms, so they are confused about why they are feeling unwell or experiencing emotional ups and downs. And because they do not understand the causes themselves, they don't reach out for help or support and end up suffering more than they have to. For example, you may suddenly find yourself unable to control your emotions, getting irritated for no apparent reason, and taking it out on a family member, even though you know very well that this isn't the kind of person you really are. This type of trial often awaits us in our forties.

FIFTIES:
A Period When We Are Met
with the Reality of Aging

Age fifty is said to be the threshold of old age. Personally, I prefer not to use this expression, because it brings to mind an image of our bodies quickly weakening. But in reality, it is true that during this period of life, our hair increasingly goes gray, and some of us may start losing our hair. If you run into an old friend that you haven't seen in ages, you may not even recognize him because his thinning hair makes him look so different—you may even wonder what happened to him to change so much.

Even people who won beauty pageants in their twenties find themselves losing the fight against aging in their fifties. Struggling to resist the course of nature, they may wear thick make-up or dress younger than their age. But sooner or later, they realize that the latest fashions for the young are no longer fitted to their age or their weight, and they start going to a different section of a department store that carries clothes in bigger sizes for older people.

Through realizations like this, we face the harsh reality that we are past the halfway point in life. We become keenly aware that we are now on a downward slope in life. We feel the winds of autumn blowing through our lives, signaling us to prepare for the harsh winter to come. We lament the brevity of life and may feel like giving up. But we can't let this forlorn feeling take over our lives. Instead, we have to remind ourselves that this is the time to rev up our engines once again, hit the gas pedal, and keep moving forward persistently.

SIXTIES:
A Period When We Struggle with the Gap between Subjective and Objective Evaluations of Ourselves

What happens when we reach our sixties? We feel that we can still keep up with everyone else, but others see things differently: the more enthusiastic we become, the more distant others become. We may endure a cold shoulder from those around us because of the big gap between our subjective evaluations of our abilities and others' objective opinions about our competence. You may be surrounded by kind-hearted people who offer you praise and compliments, but accepting all this at face value may lead you to overlook the probability that in many cases they are simply offering you words of encouragement.

An example may be a business magnate in his sixties who goes golfing with his entourage, who flatter him, saying how impressed they are by his dynamic and professional golf swings and by the distance his ball travels. They are likely saying this to win his favor, when in fact they are going easy on him to let him win. But the magnate himself does not realize that the people around him are adjusting their play to make him feel good about himself and think that he can still play pretty well. This is the kind of situation that those in their sixties find themselves in.

In their day-to-day work, they start losing sharpness in their business acumen. People may pay them respect because their air of dignity makes them appear competent at their jobs. But they have to open their eyes to the probability that people are feigning attention while really only listening half-heartedly. In our sixties, even though people might show us respect, they are probably not doing what we have told them to do but are instead doing whatever they think is best according to their own judgment. This is a period when we often struggle with the discrepancy between our self-assessment and objective evaluations of our competence, and coming to this realization can indeed be painful.

SEVENTIES:
A Period When We Struggle with
Increased Arrogance and Discontent

When we reach age seventy, we enter the winter of life. It is a season when cold, harsh winds start blowing, stripping the trees bare of foliage. This battle against the force of nature is a desperate fight.

When we reach our seventies, most of us have already retired. But a few of us will still be active on the front lines. Among them are often business owners who started and run their own companies. These people often feel energetic and intend to keep working until they are one hundred years old. But their enthusiasm usually does not compensate for their declining capabilities.

This is also a period when we develop a strong tendency to boast about our past achievements. If you look around and observe people in their seventies, you will see that many of them, especially those who achieved a certain level of success, would be happy to keep bragging about themselves forever.

What happens to those who don't have much to brag about? These people often find themselves grumbling about external factors that they believe have caused their predicament, since it's too painful for them to think that they are responsible for it themselves. They often put the blame on a family member, for example, accusing their parents of treating their siblings with favoritism. They may also attribute their undesirable circumstances to their spouse.

In our seventies, we are prone to being assailed by either arrogance or discontent, which often results in boasting or complaining. This can really be a tough period when it becomes extremely difficult to see ourselves objectively. To make matters worse, those around us are typically reluctant to tell us what they really think about us, often out of consideration for our feelings. But in truth, many of them have already given up on us, thinking that we won't change no matter what they say. Indeed, by the time we reach our seventies, the preferences, dispositions, and tendencies that define our being have become more or less set in stone. It is for this reason that this period can be a truly challenging time.

Although there are differences among individuals, those who are still running their businesses in their seventies often face severe hardships. Some of them can still remain young in spirit if they can minimize the gradual decline of their abilities through persistent and diligent effort. But in most cases, our competence and physical strength start waning beginning in our mid-sixties, and we become embroiled in this conflict between our declining ability and our wish to keep pushing forward.

EIGHTIES:
A Period When We Get By Doing Only Simple Things

When we reach our eighties, people compliment us just for being able to handle simple tasks such as reading, talking, hearing, and responding to others. Put another way, this is a period when we are likely to be in a disabled physical condition that makes it difficult to do simple things like these without proper treatment or support.

As we have seen, the reality of life is that we go through about "seven falls and eight rises" through the course of our lives, which means that we encounter a difficult challenge about once a decade. And in many cases, only by riding out that storm can we advance to the next stage.

Our Lives Peak Around Age Forty

Generally speaking, up until about age forty, our life path seems to go upward, but after that, it seems to go into a gradual decline. In some cases, it may appear as though we are still climbing the ladder of success even after our forties. But this effect is like the afterglow of a sunset. Recognition for our work and achievements often comes well after the fact. But by that time, our performance will have declined in most cases.

It is usually in our fifties and sixties that we gradually establish an overall reputation reflecting the benefits or damage to society that we have brought about. Those who have not had enormous social influence will basically know where they stand in the society by this time. As for eager beavers who are full of energy and active in various fields, it might be difficult to predict where they will stand at the end of their lives. But for average people, their reputations are pretty much fixed by the time they reach their fifties or sixties.

We All Experience Several Key Incidents in Life

If we charted a typical life path on a graph, it would curve sharply upward at the beginning, as we're growing up, and keep rising until about forty years of age. After that, it would gradually decline on a gentle slope. This would be the graph's overall shape. But if we looked more closely, we would find that the line is not smooth, but bumpy, with ups and downs. We all inevitably experience several bumps and pits, or major incidents, that leave special marks on our lives. The key events that we may encounter in the modern world include admission to or graduation from college, beginnings or endings of serious relationships, or marriage or divorce. These major life events may also include financial hardships, illnesses, or family problems.

There's no getting around these trials and tribulations that life presents us with, because they are part of the workbook of life prepared specifically for the spiritual growth of each one of us. As far as I know, no one has been able to escape such trials. We don't know in advance what issues await us, but whatever they are, we must tackle them squarely when they appear. As we struggle with them, we can build inner strength and expand our capabilities much more than we might have expected. And each time we overcome one hardship, it will make it that much easier to solve any similar problems that come our way.

For example, suffering from illness can be a very tough experience when we go through it for the first time, but we can acquire mental immunity against the symptoms so that if we have to fight an illness again, we will be prepared to face it. We will have collected our thoughts and made decisions ahead of time: we will have already thought about how to provide for our family, how to plan for old age, and how to bequeath our estate to our heirs. If you are a business owner, you may need to hand over your company to a successor, depending on how serious your condition is. Your prior experience with illness can give you ample room to make such an important decision.

KEYS FOR OVERCOMING FAMILY CRISES IN OUR FORTIES AND BEYOND

2

Marriage Partners Can Provide Mutual Support

Times of illness can be opportunities to appreciate the value of having a life partner. In a sense, the marriage system offers us relief measures when we suffer from physical ailments and disorders. We often take our partners for granted, but when you are feeling under the weather, you probably feel grateful that your spouse is there for you, and you may come to realize how loving and compassionate your spouse actually is, like an angel from heaven.

As I mentioned earlier, we are likely to experience illness or poor health at some point in our late forties to early fifties. This is when women start going through menopause, which often causes emotional ups and downs. When we feel unwell but our spouse is still full of enthusiasm and energy, earns a good income, and enjoys high status, it's inevitable that our value will decrease in comparison. To put it harshly, we may even have to bear the hardship of being regarded as if we are used goods on sale—or worse, unwanted items for recycling.

At the risk of sounding inappropriate, I would say that the more successful spouse often takes care of the other spouse rather "reluctantly," out of a sense of moral obligation. This is probably because religion has traditionally taught that individuals have a social duty to support their families and has pressured us not to leave our spouses.

In our marital relationships, the spouse who is more successful after age forty often gains a more advantageous position than the other, and this often upends the power balance of their early days.

When a couple is young, the one who is more physically attractive often gains the upper hand in the relationship. But once they reach forty, their worth seems to depend less on how they look and more on their achievements and positions in society. So even people who were looked down on because of their "below average" appearance in their younger days can win respect and popularity as capable, mature, charismatic people in their forties or fifties if they have made their mark in the world. In this way, the things we find attractive change over the years.

We should remember that one of the benefits that marriage can bring is mutual aid. So we should try not to give up on our spouse on the impulse of the moment without considering this aspect of marriage.

●

What Should We Do When We Are Assigned to Work Away from the Family?

Another type of crisis we may face when we reach our forties is a job transfer that affects our family members. For example, if a father is assigned to a new location, grade school children are usually willing to move with him, but many older children wish to stay in their current school. So in many cases, those who take up a new job posting away from home choose to go alone.* This can be a really tough experience for the family.

It's often difficult to predict how long this period of separation will last. It could end after a few years, but it could also last for more than ten years. If it lasts that long, it may get to the point where it's not clear whether we can really call them a family. But we may have to bear that pain and sacrifice our family life if we want to satisfy the desires of everyone in the family.

This situation reminds me of a story about the method they use in Africa to capture monkeys. They fill a hollowed-out coconut shell with rice and tie it to a coconut tree with

---

* In Japan, when people get transferred to a location far away from home, many choose to leave their families behind, which often complicates family situations.

a string. A monkey approaches the trap and sticks his hand inside the coconut shell, trying to take the rice. But when the monkey grabs the rice, his hand gets stuck, and he can't get it out of the shell. All he has to do is let go of the rice he's holding onto, but he is so full of greed that he can't let go. While he's screaming in frustration, he's easily captured. This is what happens to us when we are enslaved by excessive greed.

We all have to face many contradictory situations in life that cause us distress. But the root cause of this distress is almost always excessive desire. Gaining one thing can result in the loss of something else, so we may sometimes have to give up something we want and be content with what we have. We can't have everything our own way, and if we keep pushing ourselves until we gain what we want, we may end up becoming like the monkey who doesn't let go of the rice and gets caught.

●

Being Content with What You Have Is the Key to Happiness

In the example of the father working away from his family, the family has a few options. They can choose to live together if that's what they value most. In that case, the family can move with the father, or the father can stay with the family. They can also decide to live separately. If the family prioritizes the children's education and decides that it would be best for them to stay in their current school, the father will have to leave the family behind while the mother stays with the children to help them with their studies. But in this case, there is still a risk that things won't work out the way they planned.

If the family separates because they prioritize the children's education, the children will feel strong pressure to do well in school. But if the children can't keep up with their studies and fall behind, they may rebel against their parents by hanging out with a delinquent group or become violent at home. In extreme cases, they may become aggressive and abusive toward other family members as a way to vent their frustration.

Especially in cases when a mother stays with a son who is physically stronger than she is while the father works far away, what sometimes ends up happening is that the son begins to kick or beat his mother. But the mother may bear the pain, thinking that her son is just letting his stress out and that she will have to take it if that's what it takes for him to get into a top university. A neighbor may notice that she is always covered with cuts and bruises and may ask what happened. She might say, "I fell down," and the neighbor might become suspicious, since she seems to fall down on such a frequent basis.

But part of the problem may be that the son is being pushed beyond his limits.

Desires will keep welling up inside us. But we can control these desires by finding contentment in moderate happiness, especially after age forty. We can't have everything we want in life, so we should develop a mindset of being content with moderate success. If you are blessed with something, make it the source of your happiness.

Although there is nothing wrong with trying to help children excel in school, both parents and children should know that academic achievement is not the sole measure of success. Even if our children's school records are not impeccable, signs of successful parenting also include other factors, such as a close family, harmonious sibling relationships, or a sense of filial piety in one's children.

The father may miss an opportunity for career advancement by not working away from his family—his company may decide to hire or send someone else to save the moving cost of the entire family. He may never be asked to relocate again, even if a higher post opens up in a new location later on, and he may end up staying in the same position for his whole career. But he can still find happiness in watching his children grow and being there for his family. From this perspective, prioritizing his family life is not necessarily a bad decision, and it may well be the best decision for his family.

This is one example of the seven crises or major turning points in life we are supposed to encounter. Whatever the circumstance is, however, we have to make up our minds and decide how to ride out the storm.

It helps to know that, in most cases, the root cause of our agony is excessive desire. We often pursue things that seem unworthy from an objective perspective. But when we are solely focused on getting what we want, we forget to consider how other people might handle similar situations and lose our proper sense of judgment to see if we are being too greedy. In short, we often suffer when we focus on our own egos and neglect to consider the perspective of others.

BEING THANKFUL THAT NOTHING TERRIBLE HAS HAPPENED

3

We can certainly prepare ourselves for the seven crises that we are likely to encounter during our lifetimes, but what really matters is how we can get through them.

We can also find happiness by being grateful for not encountering any critical situations that could have brought misery to our lives. We often overlook the misfortunes that *haven't* happened. For example, many people are struggling with children who have turned to juvenile delinquency. But those who haven't faced these issues often do not realize how fortunate they are for not having gone through these difficulties. They have probably never even thought about their children becoming delinquent or committing violent acts. But the absence of these problems can certainly be a source of happiness.

We also hear about victims suffering from domestic violence. Men are usually physically stronger than women, and some men are strong enough to easily pick up their wives with their two arms. In a worst-case situation, domestic violence can result in death.

To tell the truth, very few Japanese men are strong enough to pick up their wives with their two arms. I have to confess that I am one of them; I probably can't lift my wife. Except for those who practice fighting sports such as judo or wrestling, or those who have developed unusual muscular strength by working construction jobs, most Japanese men don't have the strength to pick up their wives. They simply can't bear the weight. Any Japanese man who can carry his wife up the stairs deserves a round of applause. He may even be worthy of an award. That's how very few Japanese men can do this. Japan has a lower rate of spousal violence than the United States does probably because Japanese men tend to be naturally small in build.

At the same time, many Japanese women are strong enough to fight back. If they hurled themselves against their husbands, they could probably knock them out. A Japanese woman may not be able to literally "keep her husband under her thumb," but she can probably keep him under her breech if she sits on him. That "power balance" is the reason, I believe, that we have fewer instances of domestic violence against women in Japan.

The time may come when the husband's and wife's roles reverse, and we may see an increasing number of cases of women committing domestic violence. Today, many women are taking self-defense classes such as martial arts and boxing to acquire such skills as giving elbow strikes and uppercuts to protect themselves from violence.

Perhaps, in the near future, a husband will have to be on his guard and fear for his life. And this time, a worst-case scenario would be a husband's "accidental death" caused by his wife who was taking self-defense classes while at the same time naming herself as the sole beneficiary of his life insurance.

In any case, the main point I am trying to make here is that we can certainly feel grateful that these kinds of things haven't happened to us yet. But people usually don't even realize that the absence of troubles at home is something that they can truly appreciate. I hope that this perspective helps you find happiness in your family's blessings.

KNOWING OUR CAPABILITIES AND HARNESSING OUR STRENGTHS

4

Another family issue that you may be struggling with is your children's academic performance. While some students can go on to their first choice of college, others may not. But many times when students don't get accepted into the school of their choice, it is clear from a bystander's vantage point that they are getting a bit too greedy, considering their academic competence, but it is often hard for students themselves to see this.

In some cases, the students may not be the greedy ones. Prep school teachers may drive students to apply to top universities because they want to send as many of their students as possible to top universities. The higher the number of students who enter prestigious colleges, the better the prep school's reputation will be. Since it is hard for teachers to tell who will get into which school, they have their students apply to as many top schools as possible to increase their chances of acceptance. What the students should know, in this case, is that the teachers are pushing the students mostly for the benefit of the prep school and not of each student.

Knowing your overall capabilities and limitations is of paramount importance. Whether you get accepted or turned down by the school of your choice, what's essential is to know your place. In saying this, however, I am by no means saying that you should give up. Once you know where you stand, what you need to do next is think about what you can do with your ability. You may feel as though you lack the aptitude or talent to achieve something exceptional, but if you focus your efforts on developing your ability diligently and persistently, you will eventually be able to win recognition in some field. Instead of trying to win at everything, you should identify your unique strengths and make the best use of them.

The same holds true for me. When I was young, I discovered that one of my strengths was my great fondness for reading books. People who like to read books typically have an aptitude for writing books. Put another way, those who want to write need to read a lot. If you would like to become a professional writer, your first step should be to read a lot, because without a considerable amount of input, you can't expect to produce much output. So developing an affinity for reading will help you become a writer. In this way, we should bet on our own strengths and develop them.

I probably could have been reasonably successful at administrative work, but I figured that a lot of people can handle that type of work. I felt that I had a better aptitude for creative work, so I decided to focus on developing my creativity. That is how I enhanced my potential.

KEEP YOUR INNER LIGHT LIT NO MATTER WHAT CIRCUMSTANCES YOU FIND YOURSELF IN

5

Life Is Like a School for Training Your Soul

Many of my younger readers may not yet be able to relate to the idea of "falling seven times but rising up eight times." But you, too, will go through a variety of experiences in your life, and many of these experiences may bring pain and grief. At such times, don't let your difficulties dishearten you.

We choose to be born into this world to learn. So an easy and fun life without any trials and tribulations is not necessarily ideal for our spiritual growth. One thing I would like to remind you of again is that we experience sorrow and suffering because these difficult experiences help us polish our souls.

Life in this world is indeed hard. Some people lose their parents early in their childhood. During a period of economic downturn, many businesses go under, forcing the employees from their jobs. The family business your father runs could go bankrupt, and your father could commit suicide in despair. You could lose your loved ones in traffic accidents. Countless tragedies like these happen every day.

You may find a job after many rounds of interviews only to receive a phone call from your prospective employer telling you that the company has just gone bankrupt. This kind of thing is not uncommon these days, when thousands of businesses—more than ten thousand companies in Japan alone—go out of business every year. So it is very possible that a company that offers you a job will no longer be around by the day you were supposed to start work. This would definitely be a difficult experience. Even if you decide to start your own businesses with a vision of achieving a great success, if an economic recession hits, chances are that no matter how hard you try, you'll eventually have to close your business.

These are some of the painful experiences that you may have to go through. But no matter what circumstances you find yourself in, always remember that life in this world is like a school for training your soul, and that you were born into this world not to have a good time, but to accumulate various kinds of experiences.

We Can Turn Suffering and Difficulties into Nourishment for the Soul

The truths of life are quite simple. First, we always harvest the fruits of our efforts. Second, we will receive recognition, in some way or other, for our benevolent wish to benefit others and contribute to the happiness of the many people in the world. And third, there are no hardships or difficulties that we cannot overcome.

If we can anticipate the tragedies that may happen during the course of our lives, nothing will come as a surprise. This means that we can prepare ourselves to tackle and overcome any misfortune that we may encounter in life.

The worst thing you can do is to blame circumstances for your unhappiness and keep holding on, until the end of your life, to the idea that your life was ruined because of a particular incident. What's most important is to make the effort to turn unfortunate events into nourishment for your soul and strive to live the best life you can.

Pain and Sorrow Can Foster a Caring and Compassionate Heart

We can cultivate a generous, empathetic, and compassionate heart of love only through experiencing sorrow. As a religious leader, when I see tragic events, including wars, famines, and other disasters, taking place every day around the world, I earnestly wish to help and save numerous people who are suffering. Not a day goes by without my heart wrenching with grief, feeling the pain and sorrow of so many people day after day.

Particularly in recent years, because of the economic downturn, many big firms have gone bankrupt, leaving tens of thousands of people out of work. When I think about the difficulties that each of those families must be going through, it brings great anguish indeed.

But the more I become aware of the pain and suffering that exist in this world, the more keenly I feel the need to fulfill my mission as a religious leader. If everything were going right, I wouldn't have to be here to help. The fact that many people are suffering today gives me all the more reason to devote myself to helping and saving these souls. It is this widespread suffering that makes our work truly valuable to the world.

You may sometimes get weary of life, but I ask you not to adopt a nihilistic outlook nor to give up on your life just yet. No matter how stormy or adverse the circumstances you find yourself in, always remember to keep your inner light on. Strive to become a beacon of light throughout your life. This is what it means to live with a spirit of resilience—a spirit of "falling down seven times but rising eight times." I hope you will keep this idea in your mind and give it your all to the very end.

LIVING

WITH A

STOUT

HEART

MY FATHER'S EXPERIENCES OF POVERTY, ILLNESS, AND CONFLICT

1

The Hardships My Father Suffered Helped Cultivate My Spiritual Growth

In this chapter, I would like to talk about living with a stout heart. When I first thought about this topic, I realized that it's not that easy to decide what exactly this phrase means. What came to my mind, however, was the life of my late father, Saburo Yoshikawa, who I think exemplified living with a stout heart.

I grew up listening to my father's anecdotes about the various ills and vicissitudes of his life. In a sense, the hardships that my father suffered nurtured my spiritual growth. Those stories taught me what it was like to go through trials and tribulations like the kind he suffered without having to experience them myself.

In general, people come to religion, looking for guidance and help in solving financial issues, health problems, and strife with others. My father experienced all of these three major issues: poverty, illness, and conflict. From the time I was little, I learned about the pain and suffering of poverty, illness, and conflict by constantly watching and hearing about how my father dealt with these issues.

If you only looked at my resume, you might see a man who has been climbing the ladder of success with no difficulties along the way. But in reality, I learned about the severity of life by witnessing how my parents and people around me suffered hardships and difficulties. At times, they showed me examples of what not to do. At other times, they taught me what it was that I must do. I was able to learn from both kinds of examples.

●

My Father's Struggle against Poverty in His Early Days

My father lost his father when he was only seven years old, and his widowed mother had to raise four children on her own. So my father had a difficult childhood. He used to tell me about having to look after his younger brother and walking to school while carrying him on his back. He grew up fatherless and spent his youth without a father to look after the family.

After grade school, he relied on his older brother's support to attend middle school in Tokyo. But due to the outbreak of the Pacific War, he soon had to return to his hometown in Tokushima for evacuation. His path to career success in Tokyo was effectively blocked. During the war, my father, now around age twenty, had to provide for and protect his mother, older sister, younger brother, older brother's pregnant wife, and other family members, because his older brother had been sent to the war front.

Luckily for my father, he was never drafted into the military because he was ranked in the third class based on the physical examination for service. Those who were categorized as part of the third class were expected to stand by and fight back with bamboo spears in the event that the enemy landed on Japan's shores. As a member of the "stay at home" unit, my father had taken on the duty of taking care of his entire family.

I believe that it was during the war that my father was asked to teach at a school. But as an evacuee living in a remote mountain village, he probably could not earn a high enough salary just from teaching to support his entire family. So he had many different jobs at the same time.

As I listened to my father's stories, I counted the number of the jobs he had, and there were at least twenty, but I couldn't remember them all. He was truly a jack-of-all-trades. My father told me he had to do anything and everything to feed his family, from selling vegetables on a two-wheeled cart to any other side jobs he could find to bring in extra income.

●

My Father Demanded Justice and Despised Injustice and Corruption

During his twenties, my father was active in politics. His good writing skills helped him provide theoretical backing for the cause and made him one of the main leaders of the left-wing movement in his hometown of Tokushima.

He practically served as chief editor of left-wing magazines, newspapers, and other publications, and he aggressively pursued and denounced corruption including a case of alleged graft involving the then-Tokushima governor. He openly and consistently condemned the authorities, saying that they had committed an unforgivable act that should never be tolerated at a time when the citizens barely had enough to eat.

As a matter of course, those in power did not put up with such criticism. I am sure they were determined to chase after and arrest my father. But at that time my father had no fixed address and moved from one hideout to another while continuing to write articles criticizing the government. In a sense, he lived like Osama bin Laden, who was constantly chased and kept running from place to place in the mountains of Afghanistan.

Because my father was constantly on the move, he did not own furniture or household goods. The last belonging he kept while he was moving around the mountains were the entire collection of Masaharu Taniguchi's twenty-volume work, *Truth of Life*, wrapped in cloth. But the day came when he could no longer run away while carrying the books with him, so he dug a hole and buried them there, thinking that he could come back for them later. But that was the last he saw of them. No one knows what happened to those books. If we traced back where my father went and dug around in those areas, we might find them somewhere in the mountains of Tokushima.

Seen in a positive light, the way he lived—sleeping in a different place almost every night—resembled the lifestyle of Jesus Christ. But it also resembled the lifestyles of many suspicious political activists who are around today.

It was perhaps because he was constantly running away from the police and didn't have any fixed residence that he had to change jobs more than twenty times. It seems that he moved around from one safe house to another while continuing to work. This was the third type of suffering, conflict, that my father experienced before experiencing the second type of suffering, illness, right around when I was born.

Eventually, my father was sued for defamation by the Tokushima governor and was taken to court for launching a negative campaign against the governor. My father fought the governor in the Tokushima District Court. I am not sure whether he won that lawsuit in the district court, but I did hear that the suit was appealed in the Takamatsu High Court.

My father did not have the money to hire a lawyer, so the Tokushima governor's lawyer told him to use the state-appointed attorney, saying that they couldn't have a decent trial without a lawyer. My father refused their suggestion, saying, "I would never trust a lawyer who is paid by our tax money. He is basically hired by the government. I sure don't want a lapdog defending me. I'll fight it out myself." So he said, and he defended himself against the governor's lawyer. Even though he had no qualifications or experience, he won the case with his own argument in the court of appeals.

The fact that the court ruled in his favor means that my father defeated the governor squarely on his own. The appeals court judged that my father's argument was valid and his criticism was legitimate.

This anecdote well describes the kind of person my father was. He always pursued justice and despised injustice and corruption almost to an extreme degree. He simply did not tolerate people in authority abusing their power to exploit the weak.

I Find in Myself the Same Spirit of
Defiance as My Father's

I grew up listening to these anecdotes. So even though my basic stance on various issues is conservative, I can be quite unpredictable as I do have a fundamentally defiant attitude that comes out as passion.

I usually hold on to a conservative belief that we should create a stable and orderly society with sustainable growth. But when I face impending danger or a situation that I absolutely cannot tolerate, I can turn as aggressive as a dragon in an instant. At such times, I feel my father's spirit of defiance running through my blood.

If I have to, I am willing to fight against even the highest authority, even if it goes against my interests. I resemble my father in this respect. Although my personality is very calm, and I am always seeking peace and harmony, a spirit of defiance rises up within me when I face situations or events that are completely unjust.

I remember seeing my father becoming irate at injustice even in his older days. He would fly into a rage, as if to say that he would absolutely not allow anything like that to happen. Even in his fifties, he was still hot-blooded and would often get enraged.

I gradually became calm and quiet as I became older. Although I was a hot-blooded boy who was quick to protest and speak against others, I overcame the tendency toward hot-headedness at a much earlier age than my father did.

Another incident of conflict my father experienced happened at the wooden house he used to live in before building the small concrete house that still stands today. On one occasion, the police surrounded the small wooden house. Those who lived in that area at that time may still remember the incident. They may even remember wondering where my father was when the police came to his house to arrest him. He was actually hiding in the space between the ceiling and the roof. My father really was a fighter in the truest sense of the word. He never feared the police and kept denouncing those in authority.

To this day, I have his spirit of defiance inside me. I am not afraid of criticizing something that I feel is wrong, regardless of whether it will benefit or harm me. And indeed, I have criticized the highest authorities and most powerful institutions whenever I have felt that they were bringing injustice to the world.

My Father Built His House Without Money or Collateral Just by Negotiating

Now let me go back to my father's experience of poverty. My father suffered from poverty from the time he was little. During the war, he had little to eat; he lived on sweet potato vines and flour dumplings boiled in soup. This shows how low his family's standard of living was at that time.

When he was almost thirty years old, he decided to withdraw from the political activities that he had been so passionately involved in. Perhaps those around him suggested that it was about time, but it seems that my father thought he should settle down, and he married my mother around that time.

After my father and mother got married, he built the wooden house that I mentioned earlier. He didn't actually have the money to build a house, but, surprisingly enough, he managed to negotiate to have his house built anyway.

Let me explain how he achieved this amazing feat. First, he tried to borrow money from a bank. But he had no collateral he could offer for a loan. So he asked the head carpenter he had hired to build his house to cosign the loan. This is how he borrowed the money he needed to build the house.

I am sure the carpenter was speechless when my father asked him to be a cosigner. My father must have been the first person to ask him to cosign a loan for a house he had been hired to build. If my father had been unable to pay back the loan, the carpenter would have had to pay for the house he built, and my father would have had his house built for free!

My father could be quite assertive in winning over others. In this sense, he truly was a tough negotiator. He was a smooth talker and had no hesitation about getting others to do what he wanted.

●

My Father's Large Debt Forced Him to Find a Steady Job

Unfortunately, my father seemed to lack the aptitude for business. It was right around the time I entered university that I became aware of the underlying reason for my father's failure in business: it was his propensity to criticize capitalists that prevented him from fulfilling his potential to become a successful business owner. I realized that I needed to develop certain dispositions if I wanted to become a successful business executive or entrepreneur, so I started cultivating a different mindset from my father's.

It was probably natural that my father didn't do well in business, because he had always criticized the wealthy. He opened a factory in the annex at the back of our house, but it went under in just about three years, and he had to pay back the debt for the next twenty years. This must have been a grueling experience for him.

My mother, on the other hand, used to say that it was thanks to the twenty-year debt that my father, who had changed jobs more than twenty times, was finally forced to stick to one job. So in a sense, his debt led him to find a steady job. Because he was up to his neck in debt, he no longer had the freedom to change jobs and ended up having a stable job.

My father always used to complain that he didn't like working at the office. He said that a creative person like him found office work boring. But he had to bear it, because he was the one responsible for the debt incurred by the collapse of his business. His freedom to change jobs was restricted until he paid back all the debt.

These were the circumstances in which I spent my youth. I grew up watching my parents living modestly. I attended public school and a state-run university with scholarships. I never attended a private prep school or had a tutor. We were always tight on money, but it never really bothered me, because my mother would always prepare good meals for me.

The Keys to Success in Business and Financial Wealth that I Discovered in My Youth

I think I know what it's like to be poor. Figuring out how to get out of poverty and achieve financial success became one of my main concerns during my youth. I did my research on what made successful people different from others and how people achieved financial success in business. I looked for the distinctive characteristics or mindsets that had led them to success.

The conclusion I reached was that the work of successful people garners a lot of support from others. Essentially, the key to business success and financial abundance is to do work that would bring happiness to as many people as possible. No matter what kind of job or industry we are in, our business and financial successes depend on the number of people who appreciate our work.

What do you think is the resource we need to make to achieve this goal? It is the accumulation of our diligent and persistent efforts. This resource is essential to bringing happiness to many people through our work. Regardless of which path we take in life, we need to continuously train, learn, and improve ourselves to achieve better results than others. This is one of the secrets to success that I discovered when I was young.

Another essential key to business success that I found was the ability to distinguish the important from the trivial. Whether we can tell the difference between the trunk of a tree and its leaves and branches determines whether we can become top executives. Successful business executives can instantly decide what they need to do to save the trunk and cut off the unnecessary foliage.

One more key to achieving business success that I found was the ability to take advantage of opportunities. Those who become top executives and successful entrepreneurs are quick to seize opportunities when they come, and choose the right moment to take risks, but at the same time, they can remain prudent and patient, biding their time to avoid the risk of failure and protect their businesses from possible crises. In short, we have to be bold and cautious at the same time. These are the keys to business success that I learned from my research and observation in my younger days.

My Father's Experiences of Major Illnesses

In addition to poverty and conflict, my father suffered from illness. My father became seriously ill with tuberculosis around the time I was born, and he was in a sanatorium for about a year. Back in the mid-1950s, during the postwar period, tuberculosis was rife. Malnutrition was the biggest cause of TB at that time. My father probably came down with the disease mainly because of inadequate nutrition, but I believe the stress of his failed business aggravated his condition.

Later, around the time I entered university, my father fell ill again, this time with a severe stomach ulcer. In his later years, he continued to suffer from various ailments, one of which eventually led to his death.

Several years before I founded Happy Science in 1986, my father was nearing retirement and getting irritated that the launch of Happy Science wasn't going the way he wanted. He got impatient and started a private prep school with my brother in Tokushima. But after about three years, the business went under with a pile of debt. With this second business failure, my father acutely felt how difficult it was to achieve success in business.

Although this venture ended in failure, it also had a positive aspect. I was able to convince my father to let me handle the management of Happy Science. I told him that he could expound his views on cultivating the mind to members, but I asked him to stay away from the organization's administrative operations. And things worked out well this way. So in this regard, my father's business failure was not necessarily a bad thing.

My Father Was a Man of Courage and Action

I learned a lot from my father's experiences of poverty, illness, and conflict, as well as failures and setbacks that my other friends and family members faced. With the eyes of a careful observer, I constantly watched and studied how my parents, brother, other relatives, neighbors, and people around me dealt with various life situations. As I did this, I kept asking myself questions such as, "What is the true nature of the things that happen in the world?" "Are there any set rules that apply to various situations in life?" and "What are the causes of the problems?" I was applying the law of cause and effect to their lives as I contemplated the reasons why certain things happened to certain people and the causes and events that led up to the final outcomes.

My father took pride in having survived a tumultuous life and often spoke of his various challenges with a note of triumph in his voice. But based on my observation and analysis, I think his tendency to get impatient led him to live a life of tribulations.

To me, it seemed that my father was not able to achieve great success because he would get impatient and took action too soon without accumulating enough wisdom to properly handle the situation. But conversely, this was my father's strength: he was a man of courage and action. When I compare myself now and my father at my age back then, I deeply admire him for his courage and energy.

My father was a man of incredible vitality. Although he suffered from a serious illness when he was young and had frail health, he was always full of energy and constantly encouraged himself to take action.

LETTING GO OF THE FEAR OF FAILURE AND TAKING COURAGE

2

My Father's Dying Wish to Publish *The Laws of Courage*

As I mentioned in the afterword of my book, *The Laws of Courage*, my father passed away on August 12, 2003.* My last conversation with him had been about six months earlier. We spoke on the phone, and toward the end of the conversation, he told me that I should write a book on courage. He said that I had not yet written *The Laws of Courage*, and that it would be an essential book for the activities of my organization, Happy Science. So my father asked me to publish *The Laws of Courage* as part of the Laws series. To his request, I remember replying that it would be hard for me to write an entire book solely on the topic of courage.

---

* Ryuho Okawa, *The Laws of Courage* (Tokyo: IRH Press, 2009). Every year, Okawa's lectures are compiled and published as an annual volume of books called "The Laws Series."

But since those became my father's last words to me, I decided to write *The Laws of Courage* to fulfill his wish. I spent the next several years thinking about that theme. And around 2007, I started giving talks on this subject that were eventually compiled as *The Laws of Courage*. I was finally able to fulfill my father's dying wish at the beginning of 2009 with the publication of this book.

Now that I reflect back on this process, I keenly feel how hard it is to take courage. And it only gets harder, because we become more cautious, timid, and conservative as we get older. When we are young, we can inspirit ourselves even if we suffer defeats or failures. But as we accumulate various experiences, we naturally suffer more setbacks and also see and hear more accounts of others' failures. As a result, we gradually become fainthearted and cautious, and eventually lose courage.

So it is quite something to remain brave in our forties, fifties, sixties, and beyond. Seeing how my father remained courageous even in his later years, I realized how essential courage was to living a meaningful life. As my father watched me work over the years, one thing he was probably not happy with me about was an impression that I lacked courage.

Fear of Making Mistakes Leads to a Lack of Courage

I see this same tendency among the staff members of my organization. Especially the ones who graduated from the same university as I did—the University of Tokyo—are cautious, meticulous and fearful of making mistakes.

Of course, it's not only graduates of the University of Tokyo who have this tendency. Many Japanese people who excelled as students, for example medical school graduates, are apt to fear making mistakes. This is because they have all experienced a bitter feeling of getting points deducted for any problems they got wrong on the test. They always focused on getting the perfect score, so they developed an aversion to making any errors. This practice naturally instills a fear of making mistakes.

Many graduates of the University of Tokyo are intelligent and competent people, but if I had to name one weakness that they have in common, it is a lack of courage. They lack courage because they developed a fear of failures and errors. They dread getting their pride hurt. They are used to receiving praise, so they can't stand others talking about their failures. They stay away from anything that entails a risk of failure, because the last thing they want is for others to point out any mistakes they have made.

These intelligent students who scored high marks on school exams are often cut out to be government bureaucrats, researchers, and scholars but are unlikely to be successful venture business entrepreneurs. In fact, I am probably the only person ever to have founded a religious organization in the University of Tokyo's more than a century of existence, although I am not sure if I can call a religion a "venture business."

As far as I know, the only University of Tokyo alumni who have successfully started new businesses are Hiromasa Ezoe, founder of the information service company Recruit Holdings, and Takafumi Horie, aka "Horiemon," who founded the Internet business Livedoor Co., Ltd. When Horiemon launched his business, he was a religious studies major at the University of Tokyo. He never earned a degree, because instead of attending classes, he was already busy running his business. I believe he eventually dropped out of college. These are the only two entrepreneurs who went to the University of Tokyo. If I am counted in, that would make it three, but that's still not even a handful.

It takes a challenging spirit and courage to start a venture business. But students who have spent most of their time studying to get into a top university often lack this daring spirit. Instead, they often prefer jobs where they think they have a better chance of climbing up the ladder of career success, such as in large corporations or in occupations that require qualifications. A lack of courage is the weakness that we commonly find among these intelligent and bright Japanese students.

●

Faith Is the Source of Courage

I am sure my father thought I was too cautious, planning out and checking everything to the last detail. He probably felt that I wasn't taking bold enough actions.

We become more cautious and conservative when we have a lot we want to protect or keep. When we take a bold step to move things forward, we often face strong opposition. In my organization, I am blessed with many intelligent and well-educated members, but because we are a new religious group, the members will face a lot of difficult situations in which they have to take courage if we are to spread this movement around the world and become a truly global organization.

Almost all the prominent religious figures in history are like personifications of courage. This is because people who offer new spiritual teachings are usually labeled as heretics and often face oppression or persecution for spreading their beliefs. Those who adhere to traditional teachings don't see the need for new teachings because they don't see anything wrong with their current beliefs. In the history of Japanese Buddhism too, new sects at one time suffered persecution from the Imperial Court and from the older Tendai and Nara sects of Buddhism.

It's human nature to want to stay with what's already accepted and to feel threatened by new things, so established leaders are prone to suppress or persecute their successors. Only those who can survive such suppression and persecution and persevere until the very end can leave their mark on history.

One Buddhist sect that has survived is the True Pure Land sect, which today claims ten million followers. When Rennyo (1415–1499) was serving as the head priest at the Hongan Temple in Kyoto, warrior monks sent down from the Tendai sect burned down most of the temple, and he was barely able to flee for his life. He then wandered around the areas surrounding Lake Biwa and ended up in the Hokuriku region along the Sea of Japan. But later, in the sixteenth century, the True Pure Land sect grew in strength and size and fought against many warlords including Nobunaga Oda (1534–1582). It's truly miraculous that a sect that had once almost been destroyed went on to become a powerful enough force to fight against one of the most powerful warlords of the time.

How can we muster and boost our courage? The source of courage, in general terms, is our belief in our cause. But in religious and spiritual terms, it is our faith that makes us brave.

ESSENTIAL KEYS TO LIVING WITH A STOUT HEART

3

THE FIRST KEY:
Break Through the Barriers in Life

To conclude this chapter, I would like to share the essential keys to living with a stout heart. The first key is to break through the barriers in your life.

We all inevitably face several barriers in life. Nevertheless, we can't let them block our way forward. We have to tackle and overcome the obstacles that stand in our way.

No one can avoid barriers in life. The kinds of obstacles that will appear before us will depend on our individual circumstances, including our occupations, ages, and family situations. What's essential is how we are going to break through these barriers.

We may not know how, when, or what kinds of barriers will appear before us until we face them. For example, even if I asked all Happy Science members to spread their faith, the obstacles that appear will be different for everyone. But no matter what kind of hardships you face, take them as your own unique barriers and do the best you can to overcome them.

●

THE SECOND KEY:
Acquire the Power to Bounce Back

Another essential key to living with a strong mind is resilience. We all inevitably experience failures, defeats, and setbacks at some point in our lives. Especially when we stand out from the crowd, we are much more likely to face harsh criticism.

We can't help but feel disheartened when we are denounced. We may feel at our lowest when we fall down, fail, and lose our reputation. Our hearts sink when we are humiliated or put down. But this is the very time when we need to harness our resilience to bounce back and rise up again.

Although I was not conscious of what I was doing at that time, my supervisors used to describe me as "a strange fellow who would bounce back, no matter how hard he was crushed." They talked about me as if I were a tumbler doll or something, and they actually made me feel like one at that time.

After giving me a severe rebuke, my supervisors expected me to stay docile for an extended period of time, but I obviously didn't follow their expectations. My supervisors thought that this intense training would make me so disheartened that I would not be able to bounce back and instead would become a submissive and obedient employee.

Japanese corporations often expect the supervisors to "chasten" new recruits to make them humble and reserved employees. So, when new recruits join a company in Japan, they usually receive strict training for the first several years that makes them docile and obedient employees. Capable and competent workers that stand out from others are trained especially hard until they obey their boss without question. Delegated with this task, supervisors would often give the entry-level employees intense and severe training.

I had no idea that that was the reason they were so rigorous with me. Whenever I received a severe rebuke from my superiors, I would take their reprimand seriously as reflecting my incompetence or imprudence. But by the following week, I would snap out of it and be back to my usual lively self. I remember my supervisors describing me as a "true diehard" who became more vigorous by receiving their thorough and severe training in the first year.

Japanese companies do this not necessarily because they want to hammer their new recruits. What they usually want is to "tame" their employees so that they will do what they are told without objection or question. But some people will stick to their beliefs no matter how hard they are trained to be like everyone else. These people possess leadership qualities. Conversely, those who are easily hammered into submission are probably more suited to working for others and are not cut out to be leaders.

Leaders have to insist on doing what they think is right, regardless of how many times they are told not to do it. No matter what others tell them, leaders should not yield to suppression; they need to do what they think is right with a firm resolve to take responsibility for the consequences.

Cultivate the Strength to Stay the Course until the Very End

As I have experienced at Happy Science, when an organization grows large, people inside the organization start worrying about what others might say about them or how the people above them are evaluating them. They tend to become indecisive, because they're afraid of getting reprimanded for not doing things properly.

But so what if we receive criticism? Always seeking approval from others doesn't do us any good. If you feel that you can benefit your organization, or if you find a mission that only you can fulfill, you should do it even if you get yelled at, bashed, or criticized. People may say all kinds of things about you: that you are doing it for your own self-interest, that you have a selfish motive, that you never listen to others, or that you are violating an organization rule. But don't let any of this stop you from doing what you think is right.

If you look deep within and feel certain that your actions are based not on ego or selfish desire but on your strong belief that they will benefit everyone on the whole and if you have a zeal that keeps welling up from the bottom of your heart, no matter how hard you try to suppress it, then by all means, you should take those actions. You may get hammered again and again for acting boldly, but I would like you to be able to bounce back with the power of resilience.

If I could do it, there is no reason that all of you reading this cannot do the same. It is true that if everyone did what they wanted, it could cause the collapse of the entire organization. If this happened at school, this situation would be equivalent to classroom chaos, and additional supervisors would need to be called in to handle the situation.

Those who take bold actions would be considered "problematic." But even if we know that we are "problematic," we should still try to do what we can to bring about positive outcomes by contributing to the world as a whole.

Ultimately, the strength to stay the course and achieve positive results is essential to cultivating a stout heart. And to this end, we will need to break through the barriers in life and acquire the power of resilience.

Resilience will let us bounce back quickly from any defeat or failure. Resilience will lift up our spirits and make us cheerful, positive, and magnanimous, no matter how many times we get disheartened. Resilience is an essential key to living with a stout heart.

I hope that this chapter will help you cultivate the two essential keys to living with a stout heart: the strength to break through the barriers in life and the power of resilience to bounce back time and time again.

CULTIVATING

INNER

MATURITY

CHAPTER

3

PROMOTING GROWTH AS A PERSON

1

Developing a Greater Capacity of Soul Minimizes Life's Hardships and Problems

In this chapter, I would like to talk about cultivating inner maturity. Essentially, the purpose of religion is to promote growth as a person, or to develop inner growth. And this spiritual growth is what I hope everyone will cultivate, because it will help anyone face and overcome life's array of difficult challenges that seem insurmountable now.

When you feel overwhelmed by your hardships, setbacks, and adversities, you are probably searching for direct solutions to the problems themselves. And inner maturity can indeed help you solve these problems. Developing a greater capacity of soul will allow your problems to seem smaller than they did originally. So your growth as a person can make you feel as though the problems themselves have diminished.

Perhaps it's not possible for you to live a life completely absent of problems or to avoid the suffering you may experience as you face these problems. But you can probably imagine that there are various ways to go about solving them. For example, even if I faced exactly the same issue as you do right now, I would not take exactly the same approach as you would. As someone with a different perspective and mindset, I would respond to your situation in a completely different way.

The truth is that you are often wrestling with issues that are smaller than you imagine them to be. When you see your present problems from a wider perspective or from an overall standpoint, you realize how simple and personal they actually are.

You often fail to find solutions because you are unable to step outside your limited opinions and views. Solving your problems often requires looking beyond your personal perspectives. There is a part of yourself that thinks of others and yourself completely separately as if you are a tiny, individual being. This sense of separateness hinders you from overcoming your problems. That's why you need to break out of your small self.

The Desire for Self-Protection Is the Underlying Cause of Your Limits

So what can you do to break out of your small self? You can begin by discerning what this small self is made of, which I think are the limits you impose on yourself. And these self-imposed limits often arise out of a self-absorbed, self-focused mentality—in other words, our desire to preserve our self, our ego.

The desire for self-preservation is an instinct that we also find in animals, which are skilled at detecting the slightest threats to their well-being and safety. Animals constantly live with the fear that they may come under attack and be preyed upon at any moment of their lives. Because of this, they will take all precautions against any types of threat to protect themselves. When a sign of danger approaches them, they will freeze and prepare to make an immediate escape as soon as it becomes necessary. This is the shape that the desire for self-preservation takes in the lives of animals.

The same desire to protect ourselves unfolds in our own lives, too. We look at others and sometimes worry, "What if this person says or does something hostile to me?" And when we can't help but feel as if everyone around us is our enemy, we suspect everyone. "This person could be thinking of mistreating me," we think, or "This person's compliments could have an ulterior motive behind them." Some people want to protect themselves so badly that they cannot trust even their own spouses and children. They end up withdrawing into themselves, missing out on opportunities to let their fullest potential shine freely. These people are simply focusing too much attention on themselves. Our excessive self-absorption is the real reason we feel helpless and trapped by life's difficulties.

THINKING OF YOURSELF LESS AND OTHERS MORE

2

Recognizing and Changing Your Self-Focused Attitude

So, I would like to discuss three important mindsets that are foundational to cultivating inner maturity. The first mindset is the heart that thinks less about our own feelings. We are only human, so the first thoughts that normally cross our minds are our concerns about ourselves—concerns about *our* hurt, *our* unhappiness, and everything else that involves our own personal well-being.

If you find that you are full of thoughts about how *you* feel and what *you* wish for, try shifting the self-centered direction of your thoughts and start seeing yourself from other people's perspectives.

Instead of believing that other people are the source of your unhappiness, consuming our hearts with thoughts such as "It's my husband's fault that I am so miserable" and "My children are impossible to handle," it's essential that you replace "I," "my," and "myself" with thoughts of "my husband," "my wife," or "my children." Doing this will let you gain a deeper understanding of their points of view and how *they* might be thinking and feeling about *you*. What's important is to stop focusing on your own feelings and start considering other people's thoughts and feelings.

Spending More Time Practicing an Other-Focused Attitude

It is difficult for us to achieve happiness when we are seeing things and people around us from a self-centered perspective. By an immutable truth of life, happiness never comes to those who dwell too long on their own hurt and pain.

The happier we feel, the less time we spend concerning about ourselves. Those who know true happiness don't think to use any moment of their time preoccupied by concerns about themselves. If you look back at the end of the day and notice that you have not thought about yourself once the entire day, that is a sign of the rich happiness that is presently filling up your life. Those who spend their time thinking about others—wondering how one person is doing today or pondering how another person is faring in life—and constantly searching for ways to improve the lives of others know and savor the taste of happiness.

Conversely, the person who remains stuck throughout the day in self-concern and self-regard is certain to be leading a life of unhappiness. It is only natural that we want to protect ourselves from harm, but constantly focusing on our own feelings will not make us happy in the true sense.

In the end, to cultivate a heart filled with happiness, it's essential that you decrease the amount of time you spend thinking about yourself and increase the amount of time you spend thinking about others. However much time you spend anguishing over how hurt you are, it will not lead you to happiness.

You are only inviting unhappiness when you pay attention only to how others have hurt you, when you could instead be reflecting on and feeling remorse for the hurt and misery you have caused others. It would serve you much better to say, "What has passed is now the past, and what this person did to hurt me no longer matters to my heart. But the pain I have caused this person was clearly wrong, and I regret my behavior." So, the first mindset for cultivating inner maturity is to shift your mindset from concentrating on your own feelings toward considering other people's points of view.

OPENING YOUR MIND TO DIFFERENT STANDARDS OF VALUES

3

Looking Beyond Your Personal Point of View

The second mindset for cultivating inner maturity is to be willing to acknowledge diverse opinions and perspectives. We all have the propensity to espouse the values that are personally convenient or beneficial, so it takes effort to accept opinions and perspectives that are different from our own. This aspect of human nature is related to the self-centeredness I described earlier, and it puts us at constant risk of returning to our limited patterns of thinking.

We, humans, are all different, and we all cultivate unique values and perspectives in the same way that butterflies create exquisite patterns. But there are some people who seem to prefer to stick to their fixed pattern of thinking and find fault with one thing or another.

For example, some highly punctual mothers make it their top priority to always be on time and expect her children to do the same. This type of mother never forgives her son for his habit of tardiness and never acknowledges his positive attributes. Each time her son is late, she'll reprimand him and admonish him continually. She is projecting her expectations of herself onto her son and simply cannot tolerate her son's tardiness.

It matters very little if her child is at the top of his class, keeps his room tidy, receives high praise from teachers, or is respected by his schoolmates. No matter how much excellence he demonstrates in other areas of life, she continues to judge his faults. And her husband, no doubt, suffers the same kind of scrutiny under similar standards of judgment.

This example illustrates how we often unconsciously judge others through a singular lens. We don't notice that we're doing this, because, like the mother in this example, we have always followed the same values and perspectives, so it only makes sense to us to perceive others through our own judgmental eyes.

But before sitting in judgment of others, take a moment to consider the fact that each individual has his or her uniqueness and to become aware of the diversity of human souls who live with us in this world.

In this example, the mother is right that her son is at fault for his lax sense of time. But, by also acknowledging his virtues, she can see his faults differently. For example, perhaps he has a well-developed sociable side. By acknowledging that strength, she may realize that his sociable personality has been the reason for his frequent tardiness.

Expanding our capacity to see others through diverse perspectives and to discover and acknowledge their various positive attributes is part of our growth as human beings.

Acknowledging Other People's Opinions and Values

Most human conflicts and disagreements arise from our refusal to listen to the opinions and perspectives of others. We often clash with others when we adhere to our own ways of thinking and reject everything else.

A mother's strained relationship with her daughter-in-law may be one type of example. Some traditional mothers-in-law have a difficult time accepting their daughters-in-law who do not meet their expectations. They simply cannot acknowledge the fact that their daughter-in-law is among the many women who no longer fit into the traditional notions of an ideal wife that they embraced several decades ago.

Most other people have accepted the cultural and societal shifts in women, because they have experienced the changes unfolding around them and watched portrayals on television or other media. But the mother-in-law can only think of these portrayals completely separately from her own life. No matter how eccentric and unconventional a daughter-in-law might be portrayed on the screen, it has little influence over our real-life mother-in-law.

We naturally become fixated on our personal values and ideas, so we need to make a conscious effort to keep our minds open to opposing opinions and perspectives and to find values and philosophies of life that can be meaningful and valuable to us.

●

Your Own Accomplishments Can Trigger a Judgmental Attitude

Your successes and accomplishments—the sources of your pride and self-encouragement—can often trigger a judgmental attitude against those who have not achieved the same level of achievement and can manifest as mean behavior. If you're not careful, your source of happiness can end up causing suffering and anguish to others as well as yourself.

For example, being born into an academically accomplished family doesn't always translate into a happy childhood. Being born to smart parents seems to be a very fortunate circumstance for a child because it means you'll probably be gifted with natural intelligence yourself, and chances are that you will also do well in school. From the child's perspective, however, the pressure is tremendous. She feels as though she's constantly compared with her parents' shining accomplishments and bears the burden of doing as good as or better than their parents. Children born to academic parents often wish they could find an escape from such pressures.

As parents, we must realize that judging our children based on our own personal standards and expectations is just unrealistic. What we should do is to see them from diverse perspectives. Doing this will let us recognize their strengths and positive attributes. For example, you may find that your child has a potential for greatness, that your quiet son is a profoundly deep thinker, or that your daughter has a highly creative, innovative mind.

When we expect our children to grow up into copies of ourselves, our children feel suffocated and restricted. And blaming our children for falling short of our expectations will also create distress and suffering for us.

Accepting Different Views to Solve Family Conflicts

We need to constantly remind ourselves of the importance of accepting diverse values as much as possible. Cultivating such broad-mindedness is part of our growth as human beings. We need to be accepting of those who have different views, opinions, and ideas.

The unwillingness to acknowledge the merits of different viewpoints is the cause of many cases of family conflicts. Let's return to the example of a child with highly accomplished parents. Even if the father is the only academically successful parent, if he is overbearing, it can easily cause great emotional turmoil for his family. And in this case, the children are not the only ones to suffer—their mother also must deal with his overbearing nature. And when both parents are highly educated, the parents often blame their children for not trying hard enough, making the children feel as though they have nowhere to turn to for help.

But if the parents see their child from a different perspective, they will often see that their children embody something that the parents lack. If the parents can cherish these qualities, their children's attitudes toward them can take a turn for the positive. It can be unbearably torturous for a child to have her worth judged solely against her parents' own personal measures of achievement. Parents have lived much longer than their child, so it's only natural that they will be far more accomplished. But if the parents compared their child against themselves at the child's age, they may well find that the child has accomplished much more than they did at that age.

●

Refraining from Idealizing Your Childhood

Parents usually remember a romanticized version of their childhoods. And it's a natural part of being a parent to want your child to know everything that you had accomplished by their age. But the parents' stories are often full of misremembrances, and the reality was likely quite different.

We often forget our own childhood flaws and mistakes while remembering our impressive and glorious accomplishments. And I think that many a parent can relate to the crestfallen feeling of having their own parents expose their childhood shortcomings.

When my children visit their grandmother's house in my hometown in Shikoku, they would come home looking exuberant and uplifted. As their father, I normally told my children that I was always studious, diligent, and hardworking at their age. But as it happened, my mother apparently had revealed to them a very different perspective on my childhood. My mother had told them that I hadn't actually been that studious a child and that I spent the large part of my free time outside, coming home only at sundown. Having listened to my mother's version of events and seeing them from her point of view, I started feeling that my mother's recollection was correct.

She also told my children about a time when I found tadpoles on my way back from a game of baseball and brought them home in my hat. I felt embarrassed being told something I had no memory of ever doing. There was no longer any telling whether it was true, but if my mother remembered it, I probably did it.

I also saw myself as someone who had always been studying diligently and steadfastly, just as a tortoise strives to get to its destination, and I have mentioned this image of myself in my books. According to my mother's memory, however, as a child, I studied only before exams when I didn't have extracurricular activities.

When I considered it, I remembered that I was indeed at practice every day after school, from Monday through Saturday, and our games and matches were held on Sundays. So it's hard to imagine whether I ever had time to study. And I participated in extracurricular activities every year, all the way through my final year of high school. By the standards of that time, many schools would have considered that the ordinary life of a high school athlete. But before my mother jogged my memory, I had never considered myself to be an athlete, and I began to see a whole new side of myself. This episode shows how different our perceptions were.

That was not all. She also told my children that I had been a good student but that I had succeeded because my head wasn't filled with things to prevent me from retaining new knowledge. What she remembered was that I spent my days outdoors all through elementary school, always had tennis practice in middle school, and was always at Japanese fencing practice in high school. So she explained to her grandchildren that I was able to absorb knowledge easily because my head held little information to begin with.

This idea may sound a bit ridiculous. But it was true that I saw an improvement in my studies when I started middle school. I remembered feeling impressed with myself as I noticed that my studies were coming more easily to me, and I remember feeling as though my brain could absorb anything. So in a sense, I could see that my mother had a point; perhaps my mind was capable of learning new things quickly because it wasn't already filled to the brim with knowledge.

In contrast to this, many children in Tokyo spend their childhoods stuffing as much knowledge into their memories as possible. They take supplemental courses in addition to their schoolwork by first or second grade. Since these courses typically continue to the end of high school, they usually have a long way to go until they enter college.

Cultivating an Unbiased Perspective

Each of us has different perceptions, that change how we see things and others. Seeing the truth as it is has been challenging even for me. If you are a parent, I hope you will consider your child from various perspectives and acknowledge his or her positive qualities. Many people are probably undergoing challenges in parent-child relationships that are similar to the ones I have faced. Parents would tell their children their versions of how they spent their childhood, but most of the time, they retain incorrect memories. It's almost certain that the grandparents remember the parents' childhood differently.

A lot of the turmoil and anguish we find inside the home is created by the parents' biased attitudes toward their children. This scrutiny may also be pointed toward their partner as well. A wife, for example, who has many complaints about her husband may not be thinking objectively, even if she believes that she is. Instead, she may just be comparing him to someone else she once dated. From the husband's perspective, anyone his wife previously dated has nothing to do with himself, and her criticisms are unreasonable.

We often assume that we are making judgments on sound and fair grounds, but this is often not the case. It's important that we make the effort to open our hearts to human difference and look anew at the people in our lives from an unbiased perspective.

Understanding Others' Feelings and Opening Your Heart to Diverse Views

So far, I have talked about two mindsets for cultivating inner maturity. The first mindset is to overcome a self-focused mindset by spending less time thinking about yourself and more time thinking of others and understanding their feelings. The second mindset is to accept diverse sets of values and look at the world from different viewpoints.

Developing these mindsets will help improve and heal strained relationships at home, at work, and with friends. The key is to relinquish the fixed views we use to judge others and to stop forcing others to follow our own rigid rules. If you are having difficulty raising children, seeing them from a different perspective and knowing that they don't have to grow up into copies of yourself will make you feel more at ease. We often judge others based on our own perspectives, so if you have any problems with people around you, try shifting your mindset.

FORGIVENESS IS THE HIGH ROAD TO HAPPINESS

4

Forgiveness Is a Challenging but Religious State of Mind

The third mindset for cultivating inner maturity is to have a heart of forgiveness and put it into practice in our day-to-day life. It is related to the second mindset; practicing forgiveness is essential to leading a life of happiness. It can be difficult to do, because forgiveness is a religious state of mind.

In these modern times, the knowledge we are taught at school and at work fosters the ability to judge others more strongly than the ability to forgive them. Our education encourages us to find flaws and faults in other people and set limits and restrictions upon them. As a result, as I explained in the previous section, we often develop a tendency to try to fit them into certain molds based on our own standards.

Forgiving someone takes a lot of effort because forgiveness isn't something that comes naturally. To practice forgiveness, we would need to know the spiritual Truth that forgiveness truly is a real power.

●

Letting Go of Resentment

Most of the time, unhappiness and strains in our relationships with others result from our unwillingness to let go of anger and resentment toward them. We remain trapped in these feelings because deep down, we are blaming our unhappiness on another person. Often, our feelings may be valid, and other people may be responsible for half of the cause. But, from the other person's perspective, he or she may feel the same way toward us.

Some cases of bitterness and resentment are the outcomes of tragic human events, such as a person's death in a motor vehicle accident. A father whose son was killed in a deadly tractor trailer accident may feel that he'll never find it in himself to forgive the truck driver. He may wish the driver life in prison or even death by capital punishment. I think that any parent would feel the same uncontrollable anguish and resentment and would consider such punishments to be much deserved.

But such feelings of anger and retribution will not bring you happiness because wanting the truck driver to be charged with the heaviest sentence possible, even the death penalty, is a wish to bring him unhappiness. The death of your child brings overwhelming anguish by itself, and carrying anger toward the driver will only bring further misery to weigh upon your heart.

If the father took a moment to think about the driver's plight, he might realize that the truck driver is a young man who has been working very long shifts without adequate sleep. The day of the accident, he could have made a long-distance trip without an opportunity for badly needed rest. In real-life cases like this, the truck drivers are not necessarily irresponsible people but are themselves victims of very harsh circumstances.

This young truck driver is another father's son and may have brothers and sisters or even a family of his own, and he could be living under hard financial or other personal circumstances. Unfortunately, in many cases the victim's father never considers these things and can only feel himself drowning in his inner anguish and resentment. He cannot stop blaming the truck driver for his own deep pain and unhappiness, but doing so doesn't lead him to happiness.

However unjust the situation may be, we must be able to forgive others. This world is not a perfect place in which everything works in an orderly fashion. So, at some point, we need to find it in our hearts to practice forgiveness. We need to realize that holding on to the feelings of resentment and anger will not help us find happiness, so we should decide to let go and move on. We should forgive the person we are blaming because he or she is probably already suffering from the sense of guilt and heartache.

●

Practicing Forgiveness to Solve Current Relationship Challenges

Forgiveness is also an essential mindset in our dating lives. In this day and age, it's probably too idealistic to dream of finding the perfect fairy-tale relationship; we usually don't expect to find a Prince Charming who will sweep us off our feet or a beautiful princess we can save from evil and then live with happily ever after.

Over the years, we have seen a rise in the average age of marriage, an increase in the divorce rate, a rise in the number of remarriages, and a growing singles population—and the list of issues associated with relationships could continue on endlessly.

Practicing forgivingness is essential to overcoming such relationship problems. Deep resentment and anger toward the opposite sex can often lead to a sense of rejection, fear, and distrust of all men or all women. And these feelings can prevent people from entering into a new relationship, reinforcing their notion that all men or all women are going to be similar to their previous partners regardless of how different someone is from their past partner.

For example, a man who's been rejected every time he has asked a woman out may feel as though every woman will reject him and might never bring himself to approach another woman. Men are sensitive creatures; they can easily develop a defeatist mentality based on their biased view toward women.

We need to commit ourselves to forgiving others and ourselves for our past failures and mistakes. We need to make the effort to forgive those we resent for their actions, not only once but repeatedly.

You may have been insulted, embarrassed, slighted, or disdained in the past. But reliving and repining over the pain you suffered will only keep you trapped in your cycle of anguish. Instead, you can move on to a better state of mind by putting aside your complaints and learning to forget these feelings. Or better yet, you should try to remember more of their positive qualities.

Accepting Hurtful Experiences as
Precious Whetstones for Your Soul

I myself have been through many rough experiences working in the business world. I have held myself back from writing about these things, though, because having them preserved in written form would not bear any positive fruit.

I think of those experiences and the people I worked with as having been precious whetstones that polished and strengthened my soul. Each thing they said to me has helped me, as a religious leader, to practice better leadership and give better teachings to my followers.

I myself have already experienced what atheists and materialists might say when members of Happy Science approach similar people about our teachings. So the pain and hardship my followers are undergoing in their efforts to share these teachings with others were my own firsthand experiences back then. There were many people who said mean things to me, but these experiences ultimately became precious lessons that polished my soul.

I don't gain much by telling others about the harassment and other hardships I went through in the past. So, I have always made it my policy to think of those years as having blessed me with people who taught me many valuable lessons and a company that provided me with many important experiences.

In retrospect, I see that these people and I existed on completely different planes. While my sense of purpose in life came from my calling to help save the souls of as many people as possible in this world, my colleagues' sense of purpose was that of average businesspeople who were preoccupied with earning their livelihoods and supporting their families.

As someone devoted to guiding many people to happiness, it would make little sense for me to hold on to any feelings of resentment, hate, or self-pity just because they did or said certain things to me. I realized that these feelings were emotional burdens that I needed to get over.

●

Finding the Heart to Forgive

If you look within and find that there are feelings of judgment, resentment, or rage within your suffering, I urge you earnestly to let go and overcome those feelings. Forgiveness is not an abstract notion or just a nice word we like to use. A forgiving heart is a real prerequisite for your happiness. Without a forgiving heart, it is impossible to live happily in a world that we share with such multitudes of people.

I don't doubt that there have been people in your life who went against you or that you've undergone experiences that you wish had never happened to you. But I entreat you to overcome all these resentments by practicing forgiveness so that you can find peace in your heart.

A forgiving heart will give you the most peaceful sleep you've had in a long time. Forgiving the people you resent will, for the first time, let the air you breathe in taste exquisite, let the sunshine feel like a warm embrace, and let you notice the sincerity of the people around you. You never recognized all of these things before, because the bitterness and resentment within you were making you afraid of people and keeping you focused on your own feelings.

Finding Happiness Now Can Turn Past Hardships into Shining Experiences

Previously I have said that since we can't change what has happened to us in the past, the best thing we can do is examine our own mistakes and learn lessons from them, but that we hold the power to create the future. I still believe that this holds true.

But I would also like to offer a different perspective. By improving our present state of mind, we begin to see our past experiences in a different light. If you can find happiness in the present, everyone you have crossed paths with will transform into someone who was destined to bring happiness into your life.

The superior who reprimanded you, the executive who let you go, the men or women who gave you relationship scars—all these people become the guideposts that directed you to your present happiness. Each person who gave you the necessary advice becomes a whetstone that polished your soul. In a sense, they played the role of a villain on your path to happiness, so you need to let go of any feelings of resentment toward them.

If you're happy right now, you will be able to see your past in a better light. For example, some of you may blame your unhappiness on the unprivileged circumstances you have been in. But the moment you become happy, all your hardships and misfortunes will become shining experiences. You may look back on your newly married days and remember how you and your spouse were living in a tiny, broken-down apartment and see them as golden memories of your perseverance.

In contrast, if you are unhappy now, the difficult times you have been through become the sources of your current misery. And to add to your misery, if your spouse constantly blames you for having to go through the difficulty of not only living in a small apartment, but also sharing it with your mother-in-law, then your past will certainly continue to cause unhappiness for both of you. But regardless of how difficult your experiences may have been, your happiness now can still transform the way you see your past.

Earlier, I mentioned about how my mother and I had very different perspectives on my past. And this example shows just how different our perceptions of the same events can be. Of course, I don't object to anything my mother has said about me, because I understand that she said the things she did on purpose to lift my children's spirits.

In any case, I would like you to understand that forgiveness has a tangible force and that, among the different stages of love, forgiving love especially has a spiritual power. In this world, we can find a wide variety of people who do all kinds of things and make various mistakes. But criticizing them for their behaviors and mistakes or trying to fit them into fixed molds would only make the world a difficult place to live in.

Each and every one of us has a divine nature within, and so our human nature is originally splendid. What's important is to help everyone develop and grow their divine potential to greater heights of splendidness.

WE ALL HAVE A DUTY TO BECOME HAPPY

5

Discovering Unique Gifts Hidden within Flaws and Weaknesses

All of us have not only a right, but also a duty to become happy. This responsibility to achieve happiness belongs not just to yourself, but also to each and every person with whom you share this world—and that includes people you resent.

We can help bring about an ideal world when each of us attains happiness. The creation of a better world begins with acknowledging both our right and duty to achieve happiness. And it will come to fruition when everyone, including ourselves and others, carry out their responsibility of finding happiness.

How can we fulfill our duty to become happy? It is to accept the ways other people live. We should acknowledge the different standards and lifestyles, and by so doing, we can find the positive side and strengths of each person we meet. What we initially judged to be others' flaws and weaknesses may actually be the exceptional gifts they've been endowed with.

Those Who Have Achieved Great Feats Have Experienced Periods of Solitude

In recent times, in Japan, increases in the number of cases of autistic disorders and social withdrawal have gained widespread public attention. I have examined various reports that describe these cases as medical conditions, but I still don't think they show any real signs of serious disability or illness.

Objectively speaking, it's true that some children show indications of intellectual disorder or impairment. Still, I can't help but feel that these reports only seem to be pointing out the simple fact that some children are difficult to handle. It's normal for some children in our society to be difficult to manage and to call for extra supervision and care.

For example, schoolteachers managing a class of forty or more children have a tough job on their hands, especially if each of these children is a handful even for their parents. Under these circumstances, teachers may start to think of most of their students as troublemakers and may want to think of students who can't follow their instructions as showing indications of a disorder.

The same thing can be said about those who are showing symptoms of social withdrawal. The fact of the matter is that most scholars, philosophers, or writers have experienced a period of social withdrawal as part of the process of developing their career. Anyone who has ever succeeded in achieving great feats has gone through periods of withdrawing into solitude; I don't think that any great accomplishment can be reached without going through this kind of experience. This is a trait that many scientists and inventors can also relate to. Those who withdraw themselves into solitude may have peculiarities about their personalities, but there is also tremendous potential within them.

●

A Loved One With a Disability or Illness Is a Gift to Test Your Heart of Love and Forgiveness

"Autism" has been used in a very broad sense over the years. Perhaps doctors feel that they've solved the problem when they make a diagnosis of an illness or disorder and that this will put the patients at ease. They probably believe it's their job to attach a name to their patients' problems and prescribe medications to treat them. But we should be wary of taking our doctors' word for it when they offer a diagnosis, especially if the doctor works with this sort of mentality.

Instead, we need to believe that we human beings are all children of God with splendid potential lying within us. We possess the potential to transform ourselves, and we have the right and capacity to find happiness just as we are. We have the ability to change our perspectives and, by doing so, change the way we perceive the world we live in.

It isn't necessarily a misfortune to have been endowed with a child that's harder to manage or who has special needs. Even though it may appear as if you bear an extra burden, your child could be teaching you something very important. Your child can be giving you a lesson on what it means to give love. By raising your child, you are tested as to how much weight you are capable of carrying on your shoulders and how deeply your heart can love, nurture, and forgive your child.

Especially those with a strong heart of forgiveness face experiences that test the degree of love they can demonstrate toward others who have irregularities about them, such as an illness. I hope that a greater number of people will learn to believe in the power within us all to improve, grow, and develop, and know that cultivating inner maturity will allow us to overcome the sins of others as well as our own and conquer seemingly insurmountable difficulties.

DEVELOPING

INNER
RICHNESS

CHAPTER

4

FINDING THE RIGHT DIRECTION IN LIFE

1

YOUNG ADULTHOOD:
Building the Foundations of Personal Growth

This chapter will discuss what it means to cultivate inner richness whether you are a young adult, a golden ager, or somewhere in between.

Most young adults feel focused and dedicated to developing their intelligence, sharpening their minds, and proving their capabilities. They find value in these qualities and wish to attain them. But, as they get older and reach middle to late adulthood, they will need to gradually change their values.

During our youth, we are still apt to believe that intelligence and capability are the marks of an accomplished, successful individual. So when we accomplish something that proves our intelligence; gets us into a reputable, successful company; or starts us off in a well-respected profession, we feel a sense of triumph. I certainly understand how that feels. The hard work of our teen years get rewarded in our twenties when we get jobs in large, successful companies, in prestigious fields such as medicine, or in any other occupation that gives us a sense of accomplishment.

Most people in their teens and twenties aspire to join the elite, and cultivating inner richness may not be their top priority. They often focus on becoming someone who is capable of thinking quickly, useful to others, and recognized by society. I think this is a natural mindset for young adults.

MIDDLE TO LATE ADULTHOOD:
Finding More Value in
Developing Inner Richness

In our mid-thirties, we begin the middle phase of our lives, and at some point between the latter half of our thirties and the beginning of our forties, we begin to take on heavier responsibilities, such as supporting a family. Many people at this age notice that their lives are starting to get more complicated and their relationships with others are becoming more complex.

And then, we reach the final phase of adulthood in our twilight years. Now that all our children have left the nest and begun lives of their own, we have to think about how we are going to spend the rest of our lives. This is an issue that never crosses our minds in our twenties because we are often completely occupied with our own self-development and totally immersed in a self-focused mindset. But as I said, I think that this is a necessary mindset for young adults since young adulthood is a crucial time in life for building the foundation for our very future. It's vital that we make this foundation strong enough to endure the heavier responsibilities lying ahead of us.

When we reach middle adulthood, we will have to bear the responsibilities in life and society such as supporting our families and fulfilling our obligations of higher positions at work. As we live and work with many people, we are given the chance to find out what kind of people we have become.

In our late adulthood, we may lose our positions at work, and with our children long gone, we face a tinge of loneliness and begin thinking seriously about how to live the remainder of our lives in the best way we can. And it is in the period of middle to late adulthood that developing inner richness becomes increasingly important to us.

Our youthful ambition often involves becoming wealthy and famous. Some may dream about being drafted into the professional baseball league, earning millions of dollars a year, or getting lucky and hitting it rich in a business venture. Essentially, the early stage of life is a time when we chase any form of accomplishment that the world will admire and be impressed with.

But from middle adulthood and beyond, we may realize that life isn't always straightforward and that we need to develop interpersonal skills to help us find our way forward through the intricacies of human relationships. This is a period when those at the head of the line in the beginning of a marathon expend their energy and fall behind the pack toward the end, and those who weren't initially at the forefront gain speed and gradually move ahead of the pack. In just the same way, those who shift their focus to cultivating inner richness in their middle years will gradually emerge and be recognized.

Those who realize the importance of developing inner richness will start building successful relationships with others. This will be a time when we'll need to shift our mentality from seeking to achieve personal success to living and succeeding with a large group of people, whether we are in managerial positions in companies or are parents raising children. We need to go through this inner molting process of casting off the values we upheld in our younger days and realize that developing inner richness will have a significant impact on our life in middle adulthood and beyond.

Only Few Can Teach How to Cultivate Inner Richness

"How can we go about cultivating inner richness?" This may be a question that you are asking now. But you probably can't find a textbook that explains the how-to nor anyone who can offer clear guidance on this subject, whether at school or at work. Sages or pundits may be able to offer you the answer to your question, but it's probably unlikely that you will meet them in your neighbors or at your workplace. It is indeed a difficult task to find a clear answer to this question.

Even business magnates won't be able to tell you straight away how to cultivate inner richness. The best they can do is perhaps ask you to give them a week to think about it, read some books on life philosophies on the weekend, and share their thoughts as they refer to the books they read. Most executives' minds are occupied with the numbers in the financial statements and have little room left to think about developing inner richness.

There Are Things in Life That Money Cannot Buy

For example, we can learn important lessons by looking at the experience of Takafumi Horie.* Widespread media coverage of a line in his book saying that people can be bought with money enraged Tokyo public prosecutors. They probably saw it as an unethical concept that could potentially lead to corruption.

Horie probably wouldn't have faced a jail sentence if, instead of saying that there is nothing that money cannot buy, he had written a tagline on his book's cover saying that inner richness is essential for everyone. There is nothing corrupt about encouraging such a mindset.

My sense is that Tokyo's law enforcement officials felt that he was espousing the belief that anything can be solved through money, and took action against Horie out of a sense of righteousness and a duty to protect society's moral standards.

Perhaps Horie fell victim to his own youthful arrogance and didn't yet realize that there are things in this world that no amount of money can buy. This is a changeless truth of human life. Money can't solve all problems in life. Young people particularly long to become rich, but the truth is that

---

* Takafumi Horie is a sensationally successful entrepreneur who founded the Japanese Internet firm Livedoor Co. In 2006, Horie was arrested and charged with securities fraud for falsifying the company's accounts and misleading investors.

there are many things that money can never buy, and this includes good relationships. Some people may treat you well if you give them financial rewards, but even so, you cannot buy their hearts. Therefore, money is only a secondary or even just a tertiary value in life. It can certainly be useful, but it shouldn't become the primary purpose of our lives.

FULFILLING OUR RESPONSIBILITIES AS HUMAN BEINGS

2

Developing a Sense of Duty in the Early Stage of Life

How then can we cultivate inner richness? The early stage of life, from our teens to mid-thirties, is a valuable time for developing a conscious awareness of our duties as human beings. It's very important in this period to cultivate the sense that we, as human beings, have certain responsibilities and to strive to fulfill these responsibilities.

Human beings are all essentially social creatures, and we cannot survive alone. As full members of society we have certain duties that we must carry out, including both professional and private duties—whether they are neighborly social responsibilities or family responsibilities to our parents and children.

Those who were able to build a clear sense of their responsibilities in young adulthood and made their best efforts to fulfill them can succeed in cultivating a strong inner foundation in the end. The lives of these people don't crumble easily.

●

A Sense of Integrity Develops into Inner Richness

From the outside, it is difficult to tell the difference between those who have lived with a sense of duty from an early age and those who have not. While we're still under thirty-five or so, this attribute seems to have not much to do with our successes or failures. Sometimes, it looks as though a sense of duty works in the opposite direction of success. There are numerous cases in which those who are trying to fulfill their duties as human beings look foolish and those who ignore responsibilities and live as their hearts please them seem to be taking the route to a full, successful life.

But we've all learned from the lesson of the ant and the grasshopper. In the classic fable, the ant survives the harsh winter, but the grasshopper perishes. Like the ant, people who live their lives trying to fulfill a deep sense of obligation toward society are those who have a solid basis from which to develop virtue.

To live with this same sense of moral obligation, you need to carry out your duties of the position you are in, for example, as a parent or teacher. If you are a public official, your duty is to serve your country's citizens while firmly holding onto a constant wish to contribute to the whole society. And someone who has been fulfilling his duty with a fair and selfless attitude should not receive the same outcomes in their career or lives as someone who sees his job as an easy job with many holidays and slacks off because he believes that having a small salary gives him the right to do so.

The same idea holds true for schoolteachers. Consider a teacher who puts her heart into nurturing her students into outstanding adults, in hopes that they will grow up to serve the social good and find joy and fulfillment in their lives. Now consider a teacher who only works for her salary's worth and does all she can to avoid extra work without getting fired. Something would not be right with society if these two teachers were rewarded with the same outcomes in the later phases of their lives. Such unfairness in society is simply unacceptable.

We all live under the same spiritual laws of cause and effect, and we will all eventually reap what we have sown. Sometimes, the fruits of our labor don't clearly appear while we are still in early and middle adulthood. And this is why those who take the easy path—those who take advantage of their freedom in a negative way, allowing themselves to become corrupt and apathetic toward their human responsibilities—may sometimes seem to be enjoying greater benefits than those who embrace their responsibilities.

But those who have exercised their freedom to fulfill their duties and responsibilities one by one will lay a strong groundwork for their lives and eventually reap the fruits of these efforts in their later lives. These people build a proper sense of self-respect because they know that they have been honest with themselves. This type of self-respect does not hurt others or negatively affect the society because it comes from knowing that they have been true to their sense of integrity and lived sincerely and honestly.

A clear sense of self-confidence that we have lived with integrity allows us to nurture a generous and magnanimous heart. Sensing and fulfilling our duties and responsibilities in the early stage of life will let us appreciate the value of inner richness later in life.

The Desire for Evading Responsibility Is Part of a Defense Mechanism

During early adulthood, many people would prefer to escape from their duties and evade responsibility as much as possible. We can get a sense of what this is like by thinking about how children often behave. Many children dislike it when their parents give them duties and responsibilities to fulfill. They don't want to listen to their parents, but they insist upon their rights and feel no qualms about pleading for an allowance. They can find many rights to claim, but they try to evade their responsibilities as soon as their parents mention them. They might suddenly get up and leave the house or try to talk their way out of meeting these responsibilities by eloquently explaining how these are the parents' duties and not the children's.

In a sense, this is a behavior that arises from the wish to protect oneself. In their efforts to help their children develop their intelligence, parents often send their children to good schools and hire tutors. But these "smart" children use their intelligence in the wrong way—to defend their self-interest. This instinct for self-protection is similar to the instinct to protect ourselves from danger, which is an inherent defense mechanism we find in animals. Using our intelligence to protect only our personal gain, to place blame on, criticize, or offend others, will cause trouble to others and could lead us off the right track in life.

If our children begin to use their cleverness to line up excuses to evade their duties and responsibilities, it's important that we, as parents, realize that this is not the mindset our children should cultivate through life. Whether their lives will result in positive or negative outcomes depends on whether or not they choose to live responsibly. Finding a way to evade responsibility may seem beneficial to them at first, but this mentality can lead them to regretful outcomes in the long run. Therefore, it is truly valuable for everyone to know and educate their children about the importance of cultivating a sense of duty and responsibility.

●

It's Essential to Instill a Self-Disciplined Spirit in Children

The spirit of self-discipline is an especially important quality to instill in our children. There are basically two types of people in the world: those who are self-reliant and those who depend on others. The first type of children can discipline themselves; they know and do what they need to do without the need for instruction from a parent or teacher.

But the second type of children lacks a self-disciplined spirit. For example, when a child forgets to bring her homework to school, she may blame her mother for putting her homework away somewhere she wouldn't see it in the morning. She may even try to place the blame on her teacher, insisting that it was the teacher's fault for not reminding the students at the end of the day to bring their homework the next day when the teacher is fully aware that young children are forgetful. Cultivating this kind of sophistry to attribute fault to others will not help children at all. Parents need to guide their children so that they can develop a sense of discipline and responsibility.

A dependent child may also blame his parents for not waking him up in the morning to arrive at school on time. In this way, children will probably come up with various excuses to evade their responsibilities, but in the end, we, as parents, need to guide our children to understand the importance of holding themselves accountable for their actions. Developing a spirit of self-discipline is vital to rising above the crowd. Those who are capable of disciplining themselves already have the potential to become greater than the average person.

A Lack of Self-Disciplined Spirit Can Cause Self-Destructive Behaviors

Those who are dependent on others require constant supervision and guidance from others about what it is that they need to do.* For example, children who pass their entrance exams with their parents' all-out support often start failing in their studies when they enter junior high school. This is because parents often have difficulty keeping up with the junior high

---

* In Japan, some students choose to take entrance exams to be accepted into a junior high school, and this examination period is often a time of endeavor not only for the children but also for the parents.

school curriculum and can't follow what their children are learning, so they can no longer help with their studies.

The children still remember their past glorious achievements and continue to hold onto this self-image of an outstanding student. But without their parents' help, they find themselves at a loss as to what to do. The students find their grades plunge, begin receiving warnings from teachers, and develop an inferiority complex toward their classmates that do well on their own.

These children often begin to misbehave and get into trouble, all out of a desire to draw attention to themselves. They have to be always at the top, or be in the spotlight, so they may try to achieve this by becoming the lead trouble-maker at school and exerting a bad influence on classmates. For example, they may brag about how they are already drinking beer at home and invite their classmates to their house and offer them beer. They start involving other students to drink with them at the age of twelve or thirteen. These youthful misdemeanors may lead to more audacious behaviors. Eventually, they get caught drinking beer and end up getting suspended from school or expelled altogether. This is one example of how a lack of self-reliance manifests as a destructive form of self-development.

As a parent, it's natural to want to give all the possible care you can give your child, and this is fine in the beginning. Gradually, however, you will want to release your hold to allow your child to carry out his responsibilities by himself. You will need to guide him to become a self-reliant person. You may feel empty inside at first, because being heavily involved in your child's life seems like a more loving way of parenting. But if you truly love your child, you need to raise him to become a self-disciplined person who can be responsible for himself.

DEVELOPING A SENSE OF FAIRNESS AND SELFLESSNESS

3

Avoid Excessively Blaming Others and Ourselves

In a similar vein, people can be grouped into two types: Blamers and self-punishers. Neither type is ideal, but blamers put blame on others, and self-punishers blame themselves.

Blamers have a habit of falsely shifting blame onto others instead of taking responsibility for themselves, and we can find many people who fall into this tendency. The blamer mentality has nothing to do with how intelligent a person is. They try to protect themselves by attributing fault not to themselves, but to things outside themselves. Intelligent blamers can be especially difficult to deal with. They can manage to evade responsibility every time because of how shrewdly they develop logical arguments that point the finger at others instead of themselves.

Self-punishers, on the other hand, often overly blame themselves. Self-punishers have a fragile aspect to their character and struggle constantly with self-torment, often holding themselves to blame for anything that goes wrong. They torment themselves with feelings of guilt and shame and spiral into abjection. This mentality is prone to developing into depression, which can cause trouble not just for themselves but for others as well.

It is very important to avoid either of these extremes—blaming and self-punishing—so we can instead take a meaningful path to personal growth.

Cultivating a Heart of Fairness Promotes Inner Growth

At Happy Science, our teachings are based on the Exploration of the Right Mind. And as human beings, I believe it's essential that we constantly strive to judge and treat others fairly and selflessly.

Through the course of our lives, we build various types of relationships with our friends, teachers, schoolmates, siblings, and parents. And our growth as a human being can be measured by how selflessly and fairly we have been able to see these people, regardless of whether or not doing so will benefit ourselves. When we approach others with this mindset, we can improve our relationships with friends and family.

In contrast, if we constantly crave recognition and personal gain for ourselves, our friends and family will want to pull away from us. They feel less motivated to spend time with us, because their energy gets drained from constantly being expected to give approval and praise.

This is why we should always strive to take an impartial attitude. Whether or not we can develop such a mindset depends on the efforts we make. By continuing our efforts over the course of ten, twenty, and thirty years, while holding onto our wish to become a fair and selfless person, we can gradually develop a spirit of impartiality.

●

Learning from a Japanese Revolutionary Hero

The truly impartial attitude, when it is held constantly and enduringly, has the power to win over even the hearts of our enemies. Takamori Saigo—a Japanese samurai and leader of the Meiji Restoration— is a good example of someone whose impartial attitude won the trust of his enemies. The Meiji Restoration in Japan was essentially a conflict between the restoration forces—those who supported the country's return to direct imperial government—and the shogunate forces who supported the then-presiding Shogun of Japan, Yoshinobu Tokugawa. When the tide of battle began to shift in favor of the pro-restoration forces—who considered themselves the imperial army—and the shogunate army became weak, the imperial army, with the imperial standard raised high, marched north to set siege upon the pro-shogunate forces of the northeastern feudal domains.

During this campaign, the imperial army also besieged the Shonai domain. When the imperial army defeated the Shonai forces, Takamori Saigo gave out orders not to confiscate the enemy's swords, even though that's what was customary for victors in battle, but instead to treat the enemy forces with respect and not humiliate them or hurt their pride as samurais by taking away their swords. As a result, not only were the defeated forces allowed to keep their swords, but Saigo's own men disarmed themselves to walk amongst the enemy, creating a remarkable scene of calm between two foes.

Saigo had known that the Shonai forces fought out of their sense of duty to the shogunate and had been on the side of ruling authority, the ruling righteous, until only recently. In Saigo's mind, these were not men of hostile or vile spirit but men who were going through the great changes of the times. Although Saigo was on the opposite side, fighting for change and revolution, he knew that his victory just meant that the country was undergoing a change in his favor and against theirs.

Saigo treated the Shonai leader with such respect, in words as well as in behavior, that you wouldn't have been able to tell that Saigo was the victor. It's normal for the winning forces to behave as they please and create a scene, knowing that the defeated side cannot object to anything they do. But Saigo's spirit of self-control and respect toward his enemy earned the trust of many of the Shonai men. Eventually, the Shonai people preserved many of Saigo's words and teachings in writing, and a collection of his words, entitled *Nanshuo Ikun* ("Teachings of the Venerable Nanshu, Saigo"), still survives today in the Shonai region.

Years later, Saigo fought in another struggle, this time against the new imperial government, where he was faced with defeat and ended up taking his own life. In the meantime, young men from Shonai had become his disciples. These disciples chose to accompany him and perished with him.

Arriving at a fair judgment of good or evil requires an understanding of many perspectives, which makes it a difficult task. But as an individual, it is important to be fair to everyone. The truly exceptional do not allow their pride to balloon into arrogance and conceit in victory or to treat the defeated with unkindness.

We all go through wins and defeats in various areas of life, including sports competitions such as boxing, baseball, fencing, and judo and the competitive cultures of corporate and academic settings. There are many who, when they gain the upper hand or rise to higher positions, begin to treat others unkindly and cruelly, vilifying the weak. Even among children, such abusive behaviors are rampant. But these people are unworthy of respect.

Those who are on the winning side need to treat those on the losing side with a spirit of humbleness and compassion. I believe it is essential that we practice a constant, abiding heart of fairness toward others regardless of where we stand.

●

A Greathearted Character Has the Power to Turn Foes into Friends

Fulfilling your duties, cultivating a sense of responsibility and fairness toward others as well as maintaining an impartial attitude will gradually increase the brightness of your soul. Your true essence will reveal its shine to others and can no longer be obscured, and people around you will begin to notice the brilliance of your soul.

If you're still young, you should focus on carrying out your duties and responsibilities. It's very important, while you are still blessed with freedom, to fulfill your duties.

As you get older, the breadth and depth of your life experiences will grow, and so will your financial wealth. You'll gain a higher social status and take on more important roles at work which will give you greater authority to manage and direct other people. At such times, it becomes vital that you treat the people around you with a fair and impartial attitude and look at them from a higher perspective—with the eyes and heart of God as your own. The efforts you put into doing this will broaden the capacity of your heart and character, increase the brightness of your inner light, and ultimately lead your soul to grow.

For example, when you rise to a managerial position in your company and face criticisms from your subordinates, you may have a difficult time accepting their opinions with a calm mind. When you find your mind in turmoil in these situations, you must remind yourself that someone of true capacity and magnanimity of heart would accept constructive criticism and humbly amend their mistakes, thereby drawing the hearts of others, even their enemies, to them. So what is important is to develop a character that will inspire your enemies to follow you.

KNOWING WHEN TO PASS THE TORCH

4

Recognizing When It's Time to Pass Your Duties on to Others

An essential attitude to cultivate during the golden years of life is a willingness to withdraw from the front lines at the appropriate timing. I surely pray for everyone to be in vibrant condition all throughout the sunset years of life. In fact, at Happy Science, we offer many services, seminars, and gatherings to encourage everyone to aim to become centenarians. In our work lives, however, we bear certain responsibilities to society. When we work among many other people, we have to fulfill our professional responsibilities to our company or the organization we work for. So it's essential that we make sure our abilities are in proportion to the weight of our responsibilities.

If the effects of aging are perceptibly hampering our day-to-day work, we should consider retreating from the front lines of work. This is an issue that we will face in our later years. And when the time comes, we may have to consider taking a less demanding position in the company or a different job that we'd be better suited for. The decision to step down or retire is also one of the essential keys to fulfilling our social and professional duties.

Retirement is a very difficult decision for anyone to have to make. As we grow older, our egos generally grow larger, making it difficult to let go of the attachments to our authority and entitlements.

A lack of objective self-awareness often makes us believe in the illusion that our capabilities are advancing with us as we progress from our fifties to our seventies, when in fact our competence has actually retrogressed since the previous year. Those around us notice the effects of our decline, but we refuse to accept the reality. And eventually, it becomes hard for others to pick up the pieces after us.

In some Asian cultures influenced by Confucian thought, such as Japan, there is also the tradition of respecting elders, so those who are younger rarely treat those above them harshly, which is another reason many people feel it's okay to remain in their position or role. For example, a mother may never stop nagging her daughter about the same things she's been telling her to do since day one, even if the daughter is now capable of living independently on her own. Or an elderly CEO may refuse to resign his position even well after his prime, to the detriment of his subordinates and business.

Knowing when it's time to withdraw from your position is difficult indeed, but you need to know that demonstrating a willingness to let go is the last shining moment of your life. The ability to withdraw oneself at the right time is an extension of the spirit of fairness and selflessness that I discussed earlier.

When you begin to notice that you're making errors and that something about yourself doesn't feel the same as it used to, you need to make the decision to pass your responsibilities on to someone else. The same holds true when your subordinates show signs of growth and the ability to handle more important jobs—you want to pass your work on to them. My advice to those in the golden years of life is to know your place and withdraw yourself to the position or the job you can handle with your current capability.

Preparing for the Golden Years in Your Forties

I haven't been able to offer enough teachings on when to remain in your position and when to resign. Either way, I believe it is essential that we stay healthy and active as long as we can. But we also need to know that our capabilities normally start to decline in our forties. So in the years leading up to our golden years, we should make an effort to refresh and further develop our knowledge and skill sets.

One year of renewing our abilities can help us continue for five to ten more years. But if we stop cultivating ourselves, we will start seeing a decline in our abilities before long. So it's vital to learn new things and refresh our abilities now and then to keep up with the times as much as possible. Our knowledge and skills become outdated as a matter of course, so we should try to make friends with younger people and keep learning new things.

In the end, though, we cannot escape facing our final limit, and we need to be prepared for our retirement. When the time comes, we may have to ask to be moved to a position that suits our capabilities, or if we can't find any available position in the company, we would have to start thinking about our second lives. We would like to be the ones to decide when to retire, rather than being asked to do so by someone else. We will need to prepare ourselves for further phases of our twilight years, even third and fourth lives. And cultivating a fair and selfless attitude will enable us to resign ourselves properly and gracefully.

OFFERING WORDS OF COMMENDATION WITH A SINCERE HEART

5

Practicing the Spirit of Commendation Increases Your Caliber

Another essential attitude we must develop is a spirit of commendation. Often, we let a heart of boastfulness, judgment, and disparagement get the better of us, particularly as we enter later adulthood. It's understandable that this happens to us because those who come after us seem still underqualified and not fully competent, which is often the case. If you have ever felt apprehensive about handing over your job to them, it's not necessarily coming from a nasty heart. Your subordinates are still young novices, with a long way to go until they are truly ready to fulfill your role.

At the same time, if you realize that your perceptions get clouded and your words grow disparaging and critical, it will be important to consciously shift your mindset toward commending others. Offering others praise is a valuable and essential life practice, especially to encourage the growth of younger people. Words of commendation can help them develop their capabilities and aim higher; in contrast, disparaging them can stunt their progress.

A spirit of commendation is truly a sign of a big-hearted person. Developing a willingness to praise others is an essential practice for you to cultivate a magnanimous heart.

●

Giving Out Praise Opens People's Hearts to You

We often resist the thought of praising others, even when we are genuinely impressed by their hard work and accomplishments, because we somehow feel that it means admitting our own defeat. But, of course, we all know that holding back from commending others for their efforts is not the ideal attitude to practice. Anyone who has accomplished exceptional work deserves our praise, and our praise may actually encourage them to open their hearts to us.

Having high status, exceptional ability, and financial wealth often leads people to adopt a cautious, restrained attitude toward others, so people with these qualities are typically very private and socially reserved. They mostly keep their thoughts and feelings to themselves, because they believe that they need to depend on their own ability to succeed. So if you notice someone like this who has achieved something truly commendable, find the heart within you to give them words of praise. Giving praise is something we all can do, no matter our position or role, even if we see them as "above" us.

For example, it's only natural that a small income makes it nearly impossible to make large donations to charities. But even if we don't earn enough to donate a large sum of money, we can still give words of praise to someone who has made huge contributions. Doing so won't offend them; it will make them feel appreciated. They may remember us for recognizing their efforts and offer us valuable advice to support our success some day. The spirit of commendation is a quality of heart that can be practiced by all people in any position or role in society and regardless of their age.

Offering Compliments Can Help Atone for Your Past Disparagements

Another positive outcome of practicing a spirit of commendation is its power to amend the disparaging things you have said about others over the course of your life. I don't think that anyone has been through life without ever complaining about, vilifying, or slandering someone else.

If you look back at the times you criticized and put down others, you may feel a tinge of terror in your heart when you imagine yourself confessing in the afterlife all the things you have said to others during your lifetime. Perhaps you recall so many such times that it terrifies you to think that you might have said more nasty things than you can remember. If you take the time to write down all the negative remarks you made about others, you might be able to easily fill an entire notebook with such words.

In comparison, you'll probably find it difficult to fill a notebook with words of praise you offered to others. If, in the afterlife, you are asked to show both your notebooks of disparagement and praise, you may have to submit several notebooks filled with abusive words but only have one line in the notebook of praise. Upon reviewing your notes, you might want to request further soul training for a chance to amend your attitude. If you see all the words you said in your entire life, you probably do not need to wait for anyone else's evaluation, because you will already know what you most need for spiritual growth.

Offering others praise is indeed an important part of making amends for any disparaging things you have said about others over the course of your life.

It Takes Courage to Acknowledge Others' Successes

When you first start practicing the spirit of commendation, you may feel embarrassed, as though the words are being forced out of you. You may feel as if you are being dishonest. But you don't have to feel this way.

Praising or commending others takes great courage. It is indeed a courageous act. Many people find it very difficult to offer praise, especially when the person has succeeded in something they hold a vested interest in. A CEO of a computer software company who considers his company a rival to Microsoft may feel uncomfortable about expressing genuine admiration for the success and ability of Bill Gates.

A good example of someone who has practiced the spirit of commendation is Kunio Nakamura, the former president of Matsushita Electric, which is known today as Panasonic. When he became the president of Matsushita Electric, Nakamura called his rival company Sony "the champion" of the electronics industry. Since he made that remark, Nakamura successfully turned the struggling company around completely, leading it through a V-shaped comeback.

But before rebuilding his company, Nakamura practiced the spirit of commendation by calling his rival company "the champion" and his own company their contender. This was contrary to the common perception back then. Matsushita Electric had been the leader of Japan's electronics, and Sony had appeared later as a competitor. Sony was often considered a guinea pig for Matsushita Electric to watch how Sony's new products will succeed before Matsushita Electric decides to develop the same ones.

I'm sure it took courage for Nakamura to say that Sony was the champion of the electronics industry. It was probably risky to praise his rival company that way. And I respect him for rebuilding his company successfully after making this remark.

It is extremely difficult to perceive and commend your rival's capabilities fairly and openly, or acknowledge the superiority of your rival's products and services, and humbly accept your lack of competence.

●

Your Spirit of Commendation Reflects Your Potential for Further Growth

As employees, we can easily find reasons why things are impossible to do. For example, before flat-screen TVs became widespread, television screens were made of thick, convex glass, making them heavy and clunky and impossible to transport on your own, even if you were an adult male. Taking notice of the difficulty moving TVs, let's say that an executive of an electronics company envisioned the next generation of television screens as lightweight and flat-screened. But when he requests his engineers to develop such a TV, he will probably be told how it's impossible to do. Even if his competitor had already successfully created one, his engineers might still come up with explanations of why it was not theoretically feasible for them to do.

It's important to humbly and sincerely acknowledge your competitors' superior and exceptional work and continue challenging yourself to offer better products and services. By giving words of praise, you will give yourself the potential for further growth. But if you lack this mentality, you have set a limit on your own potential to grow. Whether as an organization or as an individual, the capacity to commend others and newcomers for their hard work and achievement will let you achieve further growth. But unfair criticism and words of disparagement will only build a barrier to your growth. These are essential points to remember.

I hope that what I talked about in this chapter has offered you hints about how to keep cultivating inner richness in various areas of life, including work, parenting, and personal growth.

THE POWER
OF THE
STRONG
MIND

CHAPTER

5

CULTIVATING A
STRONG MIND

1

How I Developed Confidence and Defiance as
a Seeker of the Truths

In this chapter, I would like to talk about the power of the strong mind. A strong mind is the inner strength or mental toughness that will help us overcome the difficult challenges we face throughout the course of our lives.

In 2005, I published a book a called *The Mystical Laws*.* What I talked about in this book probably sounds quite peculiar to the majority of people in contemporary society. I've included topics that are certainly not taught or discussed in formal education and are probably difficult to discuss openly at work. So the ideas in this book are quite contrary to what many people believe to be true in today's world.

---

* The original Japanese title is *Shinpi no Ho*. The English version was published in 2015 from IRH Press.

In *The Mystical Laws*, I included provocative chapter headings such as "Life after Death," "The Principle of Spiritual Possession," "The Principle of Channeling," and "Occultism as Power." The table of contents may intimidate some readers and make them want to stay away from the book. But I did this on purpose because this book is a defiance against the commonly accepted beliefs in this world and is a proof of my strong confidence in the spiritual Truths that I have discovered.

I dared to publish this book because I knew that I had been living true to myself as a seeker of the Truths. I have never compromised myself, pulled the wool over my own eyes, or deceived myself as I endeavored to discover the Truths. I had nothing to be ashamed of in conveying and spreading the spiritual Truths that I am absolutely certain are true.

I would like to be as honest with other people as I have been with myself. I would like to devote myself to spreading the Truths just as earnestly as I have sought the Truths. I have no intention whatsoever of tailoring my message to the prejudices of the current day, bending the truth, saying only what others want to hear, or showing them only what they want to see just to attract their attention, become popular among them, or win their favor.

My stance is simple: I only say what I firmly believe to be true. So, my confidence in the Truths does not waver, no matter whether others accept or deny what I say or how they evaluate it. I simply want to remain sincere and humble to the Truths. And I believe that, as long as I have a faithful and truthful heart, those who are conscientious will surely accept my message.

I am fully aware of the reactions that people have when they first encounter the spiritual Truths. Schoolteachers may refuse to teach or discuss such topics in the classroom, and your co-workers may ostracize you if you talk about spiritual matters at work. Some of your close friends may listen to you, but others may turn tail and disappear when you start talking about your spiritual beliefs.

Defying the Arrogance of the Contemporary World

While fully aware of the societal expectations, I still believe that we should be humble to the Truths. What people today believe to be true is built upon the experiences and practical knowledge that they have accumulated over the years, but I would like them to know that it's arrogant to think that this common knowledge is everything.

By offering the Truths as they are, I am posing the following questions to my readers:

- *How much do you really know?*
- *How much of the facts have you truly grasped?*

- *Have you tried hard enough to seek the Truths?*
- *Have you tried learning or listening to the Truths?*
- *Have you tried opening your eyes to the Truths?*
- *Are you absolutely sure that the knowledge you believe to be true is unbiased?*

When you first read my book, your initial reaction may be to deny the validity of the Truths and reject them. But I would like to ask you to try opening your mind to the Truths. I can say with confidence that every single remark about the spiritual Truths in my books is nothing but the truth.

Of course, you may find that the contents of my books may sound similar to those that appear in spiritual and religious books written by other authors. But I have only included what I believe to be the Truths after careful consideration and examination. I do this simply because I wish to convey the spiritual Truths to as many people as I can in a plain and straightforward manner.

By now, you may be wondering why I started off this chapter with a topic like this. The reason is that, over the years, I've come to realize that the strong mind is essential to overcoming the difficult challenges that spiritual seekers like myself face throughout the course of our lives.

Seekers of the Truth, no matter what era they live in, are bound to clash with their societies' commonly accepted beliefs, because religious truths are often irreconcilable with the values of the physical world. Conflicts arise even among those who believe in the religious truths because spiritual teachings that were taught a hundred, a thousand, or two thousand years ago are different from the teachings that are appropriate for people living today.

The more honest and earnest we are to the Truths, the more friction and confrontation we will face. It is tough times like these that put our stance toward Truths to the test. The strong mind is what prevents us from compromising our beliefs or running away from the difficult challenges we face.

Life's Difficult Challenges Polish Our Souls

How can we cultivate a strong mind? We can only strengthen our minds through persistent and continuous self-discipline. Contrary to common belief, this inner strength is not an innate ability.

Usually, strong-minded people get recognized for their resoluteness only after they have achieved concrete results that others can see. Most are not recognized until after they've reached deep into adulthood, in many cases late adulthood, or even after their death. Consequently, when we review the lives of those who are said to have possessed mental fortitude, it looks as though they were born that way.

But what I can say for sure is that willpower, or mental fortitude, is not a natural ability that we are endowed with when we are born into this world. Instead, I am convinced that we acquire it only through the process of overcoming life's various trials and hardships.

Many of you reading this now may resist this idea, wishing instead to avoid ordeals and troubles and live comfortably and happily ever after. But facing setbacks and adversities is an inevitable part of your life. You are sure to be met with unfavorable circumstances at some point or another. You may fail in your studies or at work, struggle with relationship problems, part from your loved ones, and go through painful experiences of sorrow or interpersonal animosity.

You probably wish, somewhere in your heart, that you could avoid all pain, grief, and suffering, but you can't. You're not supposed to evade difficult times, because doing so would nullify the spiritual training that you undergo in this world. If you never faced hardship, you would not be able to achieve your intended purpose of being born into this world, which is to train and polish your soul through various experiences. If you didn't meet challenges in life, you might end up leaving this world without making much progress in your spiritual training.

Each one of us is born with unique talents and capabilities that may affect our lives to a certain degree. But if these were the only factors that determined how our lives play out, we would not be able to develop or cultivate our inner strength. We each are met with the types of issues, situations, and circumstances that are appropriate for our spiritual training, and it is through overcoming them, however difficult they may be, that we can shine our souls and develop virtue.

Asking for an easy life with no challenges is equivalent to refusing the chance to develop virtue. It is when we go through hardships that we can polish our souls and let them shine. So be strong. Be true to yourself. Cherish and respect your divine nature, and have strong faith in your true nature as a child of God.

DEVELOPING AN ASPIRING SPIRIT AND AN UNWAVERING HEART

2

Desperation and Complacency:
Two Attitudes that Lead to the Loss of Aspirations

In one of my books, *An Unshakable Mind*, I talk about developing a state of mind that will remain as stable as an iceberg no matter what circumstances we find ourselves in.* Icebergs are stable because they have a massive volume of ice that lies beneath the surface of the ocean. An unshakable mind is like the ice below the surface—it is the inner strength that enables us to remain staunch as the tides crash around us.

An unshakable mind is essential if we are to successfully live through our often difficult lives. But there are other essential mental attitudes that we should cultivate. One of

---

* Ryuho Okawa, *An Unshakable Mind* (Tokyo: IRH Press, 2015).

them is an aspiring spirit—a desire to improve ourselves.

An aspiring spirit is a proof of our divine nature. When you look within, do you find a keen and earnest desire to learn more, develop your abilities, become a better person, produce better results, and bring happiness to your friends and family or to many people throughout the world? If such thoughts and feelings well up from within, or if you can find a glimpse of them inside you, this is the proof of your divine nature.

Your divine nature is your potential for becoming like God. It is your earnest longing to come closer to God. You should cherish and treasure your aspiration to improve yourself; it is a sign that you have God's nature within.

Even if you feel that you have no such desire whatsoever, it doesn't mean that you have no potential for improvement. You're simply giving into despair temporarily, perhaps because you feel trapped by your past failures, setbacks, or mistakes or stuck on a difficult problem.

There are times when you no longer believe in yourself and feel desperate, as if you are no good at anything you do, no matter how hard you try. We all fall into a slump at some point in life, just like a successful professional baseball player who suddenly finds himself unable to get hits and home runs and instead keeps botching up, no matter how hard he tries.

You may go through a period of stagnation at work. You may feel as if you have reached the limits of your capabilities.

You may have blown a major project that you were entrusted with. You may not find the solutions to difficult problems at work, or you may feel hopeless about coping with the economic fluctuations or rapidly changing trends of the times. You may feel trapped and not know what to do when your industry is in decline. At difficult times like these, we feel stuck. We fall into despair and lose sight of the spirit of self-improvement.

Another cause of a lack of will to improve ourselves is complacency. When we are complacent, we settle for easy success and lose our motivation to improve ourselves. Our desire for success may have been weak to begin with, making us inclined to set goals that we can reach easily. Then when we have attained a certain level of achievement, we may become complacent and content with our current situation.

For example, some people may have no interest in being promoted to a higher position, which, they believe, would only bring fatigue and pain to their lives. These people may feel that a monthly salary of $2,000 would suffice to pursue occasional leisure activities and to lead the kind of lifestyle they want. They may only find pleasure in drinking, gambling, or singing karaoke after hours, and going on dates or playing golf on the weekends. They hope to get by living this way, and after retirement, they may be planning to live off of their spouse's salary or rely on their children's financial support or a government pension.

The downside of losing themselves in self-indulgent lives like this—always taking the easy way out and immersing themselves in physical pleasures—is that they lose sight of the spirit of self-improvement.

●

Have Faith in Yourself and Patiently Wait until You Have Restored Your Energy

Even in the midst of these down times, we know somewhere deep in our hearts that something is not right and that we can't keep living that way. All of us go through periods when we feel unmotivated to do anything or can't think of any goals we want to achieve. But at a time like this, you need to have faith in yourself. Believe strongly that you are a child of God and that you have the divine nature within you. Even if you have no energy right now, the time will come when you will feel recharged again—just as there are different seasons in a year and after we go through fall and winter, spring is sure to come. You simply have to believe this.

It is best not to try to force your way out of the difficult periods. The key is to wait patiently as if to fill a barrel with water one drop at a time. You will gradually be able to fill yourself with energy if you patiently restore your strength little by little.

These periods of stagnation usually last six months, a year, or maybe even three years. And desperate struggle will only add to your suffering. So remain still and patient, and wait as if to fill a barrel with raindrops. The time will come when you find yourself full of energy again.

●

An Unwavering Heart Is the Source of Lasting Happiness

In addition to an unshakable mind and aspiring spirit, another essential mindset we should cultivate is an unwavering heart, or a calm mind. When we see others getting swayed, suffering from extreme mood swings, becoming nervous or depressed, weeping, or screaming during tough times, it may feel too embarrassing to watch. But once the shoe is suddenly on the other foot and you find yourself in a difficult situation, you may realize that it's not that easy to control yourself or deal with hardships.

In truth we can transform our hearts just like we mold clay into any shape we like. Out of shapeless clay, we can create, for example, a bowl, a plate, or a ball. In the same way, our hearts can take the shape of whatever image we hold in our minds. So if you want your heart to stop swaying, all you have to do is simply tell yourself that you want to maintain an unwavering heart. This is how you can train and lead your heart to become what you wish.

We certainly don't want to be someone who is emotionally unstable and constantly vents feelings of anger, frustration, and discontent. It's all the more painful if we end up becoming the kind of person that we ourselves would feel repulsed by. But with an unwavering heart, we can keep calm even in the midst of adversity. And to maintain an unwavering heart, we need to build a strong mind. You can strengthen your mind by constantly training it to turn in the right direction.

A heart immersed in sorrow becomes fragile and forlorn, like a leaf tossed about by surging floodwaters. But we should try to minimize the impact of the biggest turbulence of our lives. Always seek a calm mind by alleviating your pain in times of sadness and by controlling yourself from flying into raptures in times of joy.

Instill in yourself a wish to always maintain peace of mind, to remain calm and undisturbed, and to diligently persist in your efforts to improve yourself. This is how you can take control of your soul, which is a sure way to find true happiness. A stable, unwavering heart is a source of lasting happiness.

THE THREE DEVELOPMENTAL STAGES OF CHARACTER GROWTH

3

THE FIRST STAGE:
Become Sharp, Capable, and Eloquent

Now let us explore in what directions we should aim to improve ourselves. In the first stage of life, from our childhood and school days through our young adulthood, we should aim to become valuable assets to society by training our minds and bodies. This is a period when we should work to become a sharp, intelligent, and eloquent person by practicing self-discipline.

In our teens and twenties, we spend most of our time on our studies so that we can develop our ability to think fast, express ourselves clearly, and accurately define and solve various problems.

Intelligent, sharp, perceptive, savvy: these are the attributes that we want to develop in the early stage of life. According to traditional Chinese philosophy, a person with these attributes is the first type of person that we want to aim to become.

Young adulthood is a period of self-cultivation when we build the foundation of our own success, and developing these attributes will lead us to become the so-called "young elite," the kind of people that companies have high hopes for. But soon, around age thirty, we need to move on to the next stage of our soul growth. And this shift begins with thinking about what it is that the "sharp, capable, and eloquent" person lacks.

THE SECOND STAGE:
Become Bold, Dynamic, and Magnanimous

What intelligent and eloquent people often lack is the mind-set of leadership. Needless to say, being sharp and capable at what we do is how we win recognition from others. In fact, developing the first set of character qualities during our school days or at the start of our career will definitely lead to a high evaluation of our work. However, we soon reach a turning point, usually between ages thirty and forty, when we start to feel that something is missing.

What young people often lack is the magnanimity that's necessary to guide and lead others. It is this mindset that inspires others to recognize us as leaders and follow us. It gives us the power to lead, accept, and embrace others. It also enables us to forgive other peoples' mistakes, lead them to correct their mistakes, and persistently guide them to the right path.

Bold, dynamic, and magnanimous: these are the second-level attributes described in Chinese thought. People with these qualities of character are more powerfully capable than those who are simply sharp and competent at handling their day-to-day work. People with these higher-level attributes have the magnetism or the high caliber that make others want to follow their lead.

Overcoming Pessimism to Develop a Dynamic Character

Earlier, I talked about the importance of cultivating an unwavering heart to keep from being swayed by the emotional ups and downs of joy and sorrow, pain and pleasure. As we go through life, we often find ourselves in unpleasant and unfavorable circumstances. Setbacks and problems arise, and incidents that work against us occur. But if we can develop this second set of attributes, we will be able to remain dynamic and overcome the barriers we face without sweating over them, even in situations that would otherwise make us want to whine, cry, grumble, or blame others.

You can certainly call this mental attitude simply optimism, but it is different from the carefree optimism of ignorance. In general, optimists tend not to be meticulous or studious. For example, if you ask an optimistic person how he feels he did on a test, he will probably say that he did okay. But when his score comes out, you may be surprised that it's actually really bad. This type of person can remain happy-go-lucky because he doesn't even know which problems he got wrong on the test.

Conversely, high achievers are apt to focus on the mistakes they have made, so they often develop a pessimistic outlook. They fret over the points that were subtracted from the perfect score, even if it was a single point. Many of the best and the brightest in school end up becoming pessimists as a result of always trying to make up for their deficiencies. This tendency is particularly apparent in Japan, where the further they climb up the academic ladder and the more formal education they receive, the more pessimistic they tend to become.

The positive side of this perfectionism is that it prevents them from making mistakes. Those who constantly make mistakes in their day-to-day work get in the way of their company's daily operations and work flow, which could bring great detriment to their business. In that sense, being meticulous can benefit the organization they work for. However, if they want to become leaders, simply sticking to details will not fill the bill. A predilection for details is not a leadership quality, because it often leads them to become obsessed with their own projects and exclude people who do not conform to their ways of doing things.

We should certainly work hard to improve our mental agility, but that's not enough. We also need to overcome pessimism and develop a fundamentally dynamic disposition. People will start following you only when you develop a positive and bright outlook on life.

Leaders should not make judgments simply based on whether or not a person has made a mistake. Instead, they must be able to see the big picture and remain placid at all times. Someone with a bold, dynamic, and magnanimous disposition will be able to handle a crisis with a smile, take responsibility even for other people's mistakes, and always take the lead. This is not an innate trait.

Although some kids seem to be born with bold and dynamic traits, they are often quick-tempered bullies who fall behind in their studies. These bossy people usually aren't high achievers at school and are often incompetent at work, because they can only do things their way.

So we should not skip the first step, which is to become quick thinkers, eloquent speakers, and competent and capable individuals. But eventually, we should aim to move on to the next stage and acquire a bold, dynamic, and magnanimous character.

●

Developing Heroic Traits by Cultivating Magnanimity

You can build up your inner self, probably not in an instant, but certainly over time. You can develop bold, dynamic, and magnanimous attributes if you keep at it over a period of ten years or more. You can gradually change yourself to the direction you are aiming for if you continue your efforts for a decade. During this time, it is not only yourself that will change. Your inner transformation will also change the way others see you.

After all, intelligent perfectionism can only take you so far. Once you develop your mental agility, you should then strive to develop and acquire a heroic personality. A heroic personality will attract intelligent and capable people who will flock around you and offer to help with your work, because heroism is something that they lack.

It's best to acquire a bold, dynamic, and magnanimous character during your thirties or forties, because this is the central period in our lives and an essential turning point when we begin to gain recognition for our achievements and climb up the career ladder to managerial positions. Middle adulthood is when we should aim to develop the magnanimous traits of a hero.

We cannot change ourselves instantaneously. Even if you hold a strong vision of your ideal self today, that vision will not come true tomorrow. But if you give yourself ten years, you will be able to gradually change your habits and propensities to become the type of person you want to be. As long as you hold on to your aspiration, you will continue to move closer to your vision. But if you lack the aspiration to grow in the first place, you'll never make progress.

Quick thinkers who are not willing to make the effort to improve themselves often become critical of others: they focus on others' weaknesses and remain faultfinders throughout their lives. Although their accumulated experience and knowledge could help them achieve managerial positions, they rarely achieve great success because they lack the capacity to lead and guide others.

It is essential that we transform ourselves in this stage to expand our capacities and to cultivate magnanimity. This is the second set of character qualities we should aim to develop.

THE THIRD STAGE:
Become Calm, Profound, and Dignified

The third set of character qualities that Eastern philosophy recommends we develop is calmness, profoundness, and dignity. Someone who exemplifies such greatness is Takamori Saigo, the nineteenth-century Japanese samurai and legendary hero I mentioned in Chapter 4. He is known to have had a gallant character of depth and tranquility.

Intelligent and eloquent people can acquire heroic traits by gradually expanding their capacities. Their next step is to develop a quiet and profound character by deepening their thoughts and pursuing insight in solitude. This is the path we need to take to acquire wisdom.

We cannot acquire wisdom if we are always busy interacting with others. Although obtaining information through diligent study can definitely expand our knowledge base, this alone will not make us wise in the truest sense. Gaining wisdom is not about constantly receiving information and disseminating it as it comes in. On TV and other media, we see a lot of mavens in different fields. Many of them are well-versed in an array of subjects, but this does not mean that they have acquired wisdom.

Wisdom can only be gained in silence. We need to think deeply and polish our thoughts in silence to gain profound insights. This is how we can add calmness and depth to our characters.

Another attribute we want to add to our character is dignity. Becoming a true leader requires imperturbability and deep wisdom, which we cannot gain if we are easily disturbed by the things that happen around us and react to them imprudently.

If we get caught up in gathering information, we end up jumping at every piece of news like a grasshopper or getting trapped in the trivial information we find like a fly caught in a glass jar. I am not denying the value of obtaining information and knowledge, but to develop it into wisdom, we need to cultivate a habit of deep contemplation. It is through this process of acquiring profound insights that we can build up a dignified, profound, and unwavering character.

This is the character of a person of greatness as taught in the East. Becoming such a high-caliber person of depth and tranquility is the third type of person we want to aim to become.

We need to develop these traits if we want to take on a central role in grave matters on a national or global scale, or in times of crisis or emergency. Undertaking such an enormous responsibility requires more than a bold and positive attitude, not to mention cleverness. What enables us to conquer critical challenges are the deep wisdom, unshakable mind, and unwavering heart that together constitute a calm, profound, and dignified character.

These are the three developmental stages of human character described in traditional Eastern philosophy, and this indeed is an insightful view of our inner growth.

CHARACTER ANALYSIS:
Why George W. Bush Defeated Al Gore

In the Western world, those who are intelligent and competent are often most highly evaluated, but in some respects, they too recognize and value more profound attributes of human character.

We can see an example of this in George W. Bush's win against Al Gore, then vice president in the Clinton Administration, in the 2000 U.S. presidential election. Most Americans probably thought that Gore was definitely the smarter of the two. With a degree from Harvard University, Gore was known for his exceptional intelligence and sharp mind. He was so smart that some people even said that there was nothing to worry about if anything happened to President Clinton, because Gore could easily take over the presidency. However, it was not the smart Gore, but Bush who was elected president.

Bush was not really the intelligent type. He did not have outstanding academic success; rather, it seems that he managed to make it through college thanks to his family name. On the other hand, Gore was the type of person who had to personally handle everything himself. He is said to have reviewed every single detail and even called people directly from his cell phone to talk things over before making a decision. Gore reminds me, incidentally, of a former Japanese prime minister, Ryutaro Hashimoto. He would directly contact the legislative assistants who drafted proposed legislation and share his opinions about it with them. He was no doubt sharp and smart, but he was also obsessed with detail.

From the perspective of human character, Bush was elected president because he had the capacity for using other people. Although he was a bit unsophisticated, he was able to use those who were more knowledgeable and competent than himself.

There is one anecdote that illustrates this. George W. Bush wasn't savvy about diplomatic matters. On one occasion, he couldn't even name the leaders of the world's hot spots. But reportedly, he remained unabashed and said that all he had to do was ask his staff for their names, which would only take three minutes.

Even though Bush was certainly not as smart as Gore, he was definitely capable of using others. This difference in their characters was probably the subconscious reason people chose to vote for him. I believe this is because people from the West essentially have an insight into character that is similar to that of traditional Eastern philosophy.

We can't tell whether former president Bush ever acquired the depth and tranquility of the third level of character development, but we know that he did have certain heroic traits associated with the second level. I believe that this is why he was able to distinguish himself from Gore, which probably led to his win.

Bush may still have a long way to go to achieve true wisdom, however. He seemed to uphold black-or-white thinking and have a high propensity to make judgments based on the dualism of good versus evil. So cultivating more profound wisdom would have benefitted him more.

Bush is a man of strong religious faith, and he seems to have close ties with right-wing Christian groups. Further developing his understanding of the religious and spiritual Truths would probably help him cultivate depth of character. This practical example shows how character development can affect us in real life.

HARNESSING THE TREMENDOUS POWER OF THE STRONG MIND

4

To conclude this chapter, let me briefly summarize the attributes and qualities of character that we should aim to develop throughout our lives. In the first stage of your life—in your teens and twenties—cultivate the sharp, capable, and eloquent self. In your thirties and forties, transform yourself into a bold, dynamic, and magnanimous person. Finally, from your forties to fifties and sixties, develop yourself to become a person of calmness, profoundness, and dignity.

As long as we take our aspirations to heart and persevere in our efforts to become great leaders, we can gradually transform ourselves and cultivate our inner qualities at each stage of our lives. It may take two decades to reach each of the three stages of character development. But the tremendous power of the strong mind will allow us to gradually build up our characters over long periods of time. We can train and develop ourselves with the power of this inner strength.

In the end, the ability to shape ourselves is the true freedom that we are endowed with and the most precious gift we're given. The freedom that gives us true joy and happiness is not the freedom to spoil ourselves nor the freedom to do whatever pleases us but the freedom to develop ourselves. And the power of the strong mind allows us to experience the lasting joy of developing ourselves over a long period of time.

Strong willpower is not an innate ability. We can only acquire it by overcoming challenges and hardships under different circumstances. We must believe in our potential to cultivate this power and aim for continuous growth as our goal in life.

AFTERWORD

When I was young, I believed that nothing was impossible if I could just be smart and eloquent. However, with the flow of time, I learned the importance of cultivating a stout heart, a persevering spirit, inner maturity, and inner richness.

At the age of thirty-two, I published *Invincible Thinking*, which grew to become a best-selling book. Now, decades later, as I offer this book, *The Strong Mind*, to the world, I realize that I have been constantly striving to be a "true diehard" who never gives up and who persists in thinking positively and constructively.

I believe that repeated reading will show that it is a good book with enduring lessons, and I sincerely hope that it will serve as spiritual sustenance for as many people as possible.

Ryuho Okawa
Founder and CEO
Happy Science Group

ABOUT THE AUTHOR

RYUHO OKAWA is the founder and CEO of a global movement, Happy Science, and an international best-selling author with a simple goal: to help people find true happiness and create a better world.

His deep compassion and sense of responsibility for the happiness of each individual has prompted him to publish over 2,300 titles of religious, spiritual, and self-development teachings, covering a broad range of topics including how our thoughts influence reality, the nature of love, and the path to enlightenment. Eastern wisdom that Okawa offers helps us find a new avenue for solutions to the issues we are facing now personally and globally. He also writes on the topics of management and economy, as well as the relationship between religion and politics in the global context. To date, Okawa's books have sold over 100 million copies worldwide and been translated into 29 languages.

Okawa has dedicated himself to improving society and creating a better world. In 1986, Okawa founded Happy Science as a spiritual movement dedicated to bringing greater happiness to humankind by uniting religions and cultures to live in harmony. Happy Science has grown rapidly from its beginnings in Japan to a worldwide organization with over 12 million members in more than 100 countries. Okawa is compassionately committed to the spiritual growth of others. In addition to writing and publishing books, he continues to give lectures around the world.

ABOUT HAPPY SCIENCE

Happy Science is a global movement that empowers individuals to find purpose and spiritual happiness and to share that happiness with their families, societies, and the world. With more than 12 million members around the world, Happy Science aims to increase awareness of spiritual truths and expand our capacity for love, compassion, and joy so that together we can create the kind of world we all wish to live in.

Activities at Happy Science are based on the Principles of Happiness (Love, Wisdom, Self-Reflection, and Progress). These principles embrace worldwide philosophies and beliefs, transcending boundaries of culture and religions.

Love teaches us to give ourselves freely without expecting anything in return; it encompasses giving, nurturing, and forgiving.

Wisdom leads us to the insights of spiritual truths, and opens us to the true meaning of life and the will of God (the universe, the highest power, Buddha).

Self-Reflection brings a mindful, nonjudgmental lens to our thoughts and actions to help us find our truest selves—the essence of our souls—and deepen our connection to the highest power. It helps us attain a clean and peaceful mind and leads us to the right life path.

Progress emphasizes the positive, dynamic aspects of our spiritual growth—actions we can take to manifest and spread happiness around the world. It's a path that not only expands our soul growth, but also furthers the collective potential of the world we live in.

PROGRAMS AND EVENTS

The doors of Happy Science are open to all. We offer a variety of programs and events, including self-exploration and self-growth programs, spiritual seminars, meditation and contemplation sessions, study groups, and book events.

Our programs are designed to:
- Deepen your understanding of your purpose and meaning in life
- Improve your relationships and increase your capacity to love unconditionally
- Attain a peace of mind, decrease anxiety and stress, and feel positive
- Gain deeper insights and broader perspective on the world
- Learn how to overcome life's challenges... and much more.

For more information, visit happyscience-na.org or happy-science.org.

INTERNATIONAL SEMINARS

Each year, friends from all over the world join our international seminars, held at our faith centers in Japan. Different programs are offered each year and cover a wide variety of topics, including improving relationships, practicing the Eightfold Path to enlightenment, and loving yourself, to name just a few.

HAPPY SCIENCE MONTHLY

Our monthly publication covers the latest featured lectures, members' life-changing experiences and other news from members around the world, book reviews, and many other topics. Downloadable PDF files are available at happyscience-na.org. Copies and back issues in Portuguese, Chinese, and other languages are available upon request. For more information, contact us via e-mail at tokyo@happy-science.org.

CONTACT INFORMATION

Happy Science is a worldwide organization with faith centers around the globe. For a comprehensive list of centers, visit the worldwide directory at happy-science.org or happyscience-na.org. The following are some of the many Happy Science locations:

UNITED STATES AND CANADA

NEW YORK
79 Franklin Street New York, NY 10013
Phone: 212-343-7972 Fax: 212-343-7973
Email: ny@happy-science.org
Website: newyork.happyscience-na.org

NEW JERSEY
725 River Rd. #102B Edgewater, NJ 07020
Phone: 201-313-0127 Fax: 201-313-0120
Email: nj@happy-science.org
Website: newjersey.happyscience-na.org

FLORIDA
5208 8th St. Zephyrhills, FL 33542
Phone: 813-715-0000 Fax: 813-715-0010
Email: florida@happy-science.org
Website: florida.happyscience-na.org

ATLANTA

1874 Piedmont Ave. NE Suite 360-C Atlanta, GA 30324
Phone: 404-892-7770
Email: atlanta@happy-science.org
Website: atlanta.happyscience-na.org

SAN FRANCISCO

525 Clinton Street, Redwood City, CA 94062
Phone&Fax: 650-363-2777
Email: sf@happy-science.org
Website: sanfrancisco.happyscience- na.org

LOS ANGELES

1590 E. Del Mar Blvd. Pasadena, CA 91106
Phone: 626-395-7775 Fax: 626-395-7776
Email: la@happy-science.org
Website: losangeles.happyscience-na.org

ORANGE COUNTY

10231 Slater Ave #204 Fountain Valley, CA 92708
Phone: 714-745-1140
Email: oc@happy-science.org

SAN DIEGO

7841 Balboa Ave. Suite #202 San Diego, CA 92111
Phone: 619-381-7615 Fax: 626-395-7776
E-mail: sandiego@happy-science.org
Website: happyscience-la.org

HAWAII

1221 Kapiolani Blvd. Suite 920, Honolulu, HI 96814
Phone: 808-591-9772 Fax: 808-591-9776
Email: hi@happy-science.org
Website: hawaii.happyscience-na.org

KAUAI

4504 Kukui Street, Dragon Building Suite 207 Kapaa, HI 96746
Phone: 808-822-7007 Fax: 808-822-6007
Email: kauai-hi@happy-science.org
Website: kauai.happyscience-na.org

TORONTO

845 The Queensway Etobicoke, ON M8Z 1N6 Canada
Phone: 1-416-901-3747
Email: toronto@happy-science.org
Website: happy-science.ca

VANCOUVER

#212-2609 East 49th Avenue, Vancouver, BC,V5S 1J9 Canada
Phone: 1-604-437-7735 Fax: 1-604-437-7764
Email: vancouver@happy-science.org
Website: happy-science.ca

INTERNATIONAL

TOKYO

1-6-7 Togoshi, Shinagawa Tokyo, 142-0041 Japan
Phone: 81-3-6384-5770 Fax: 81-3-6384-5776
Email: tokyo@happy-science.org
Website: happy-science.org

LONDON

3 Margaret Street London,W1W 8RE United Kingdom
Phone: 44-20-7323-9255 Fax: 44-20-7323-9344
Email: eu@happy-science.org
Website: happyscience-uk.org

SYDNEY
516 Pacific Hwy, Lane Cove North, NSW 2066 Australia
Phone: 61-2-9411-2877 Fax: 61-2-9411-2822
Email: sydney@happy-science.org

BRAZIL HEADQUARTERS
Rua. Domingos de Morais 1154, Vila Mariana, Sao Paulo, SP
CEP 04009-002 Brazil
Phone: 55-11-5088-3800 Fax: 55-11-5088-3806
Email: sp@happy-science.org
Website: happyscience.com.br

JUNDIAI
Rua Congo, 447, Jd. Bonfiglioli, Jundiai
CEP 13207-340
Phone: 55-11-4587-5952
Email: jundiai@happy-science.org

SEOUL
74, Sadang-ro 27-gil, Dongjak-gu, Seoul, Korea
Phone: 82-2-3478-8777 Fax: 82-2- 3478-9777
Email: korea@happy-science.org
Website: happyscience-korea.org

TAIPEI
No. 89, Lane 155, Dunhua N. Road Songshan District,
Taipei City, 105 Taiwan
Phone: 886-2-2719-9377 Fax: 886-2-2719-5570
Email: taiwan@happy-science.org
Website: happyscience-tw.org

MALAYSIA
No 22A, Block2, Jalil Link, Jalan Jalil Jaya 2,
Bukit Jalil 57000 Kuala Lumpur, Malaysia
Phone: 60-3-8998-7877 Fax: 60-3-8998-7977
Email: malaysia@happy-science.org
Website: happyscience.org.my

NEPAL
Kathmandu Metropolitan City, Ward No. 15, Ring Road,
Kimdol, Sitapaila Kathmandu, Nepal
Phone: 977-1-427-2931
Email: nepal@happy-science.org

UGANDA
Plot 877 Rubaga Road, Kampala P.O. Box 34130
Kampala, Uganda
Phone: 256-79-3238-002
Email: uganda@happy-science.org
Website: happyscience-uganda.org

HAPPY SCIENCE UNIVERSITY

* This is an unaccredited institution of higher education.

THE FOUNDING SPIRIT AND THE GOAL OF EDUCATION

Based on the founding philosophy of the university, "Pursuit of happiness and the creation of a new civilization," education, research and studies will be provided to help students acquire deep understanding grounded in religious belief and advanced expertise with the objectives of producing "great talents of virtue" who can contribute in a broad-ranging way to serve Japan and the international society.

FACULTIES

Faculty of Human Happiness

Students in this faculty will pursue liberal arts from various perspectives with a multidisciplinary approach, explore and envision an ideal state of human beings and society.

Faculty of Successful Management

This faculty aims to realize successful management that helps organizations to create value and wealth for society and to contribute to the happiness and the development of management and employees as well as society as a whole.

Faculty of Future Creation

Students in this faculty study subjects such as political science, journalism, performing arts and artistic expression, and explore and present new political and cultural models based on truth, goodness and beauty.

Faculty of Future Industry

This faculty aims to nurture engineers who can resolve various issues facing modern civilization from a technological standpoint and contribute to the creation of new industries of the future.

HAPPY SCIENCE
ACADEMY
JUNIOR AND SENIOR HIGH SCHOOL

Happy Science Academy Junior and Senior High School is a boarding school founded with the goal of educating the future leaders of the world who can have a big vision, persevere, and take on new challenges. Currently, there are two campuses in Japan; the Nasu Main Campus in Tochigi Prefecture, founded in 2010, and the Kansai Campus in Shiga Prefecture, founded in 2013.

ABOUT IRH PRESS USA

IRH Press USA Inc. was founded in 2013 as an affiliated firm of IRH Press Co., Ltd. Based in New York, the press publishes books in various categories including spirituality, religion, and self-improvement and publishes books by Ryuho Okawa, the author of 100 million books sold worldwide. For more information, visit OkawaBooks.com.

Follow us on:
Facebook: Okawa Books
Twitter: Okawa Books
Goodreads: Ryuho Okawa
Instagram: OkawaBooks
Pinterest: Okawa Books

BOOKS BY
RYUHO OKAWA

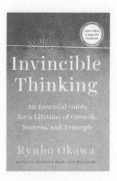

INVINCIBLE THINKING
An Essential Guide for a Lifetime of Growth, Success, and Triumph

Hardcover | 208 pages | $16.95 | ISBN: 978-1-942125-25-9

Invincible Thinking is the dynamite that lets us open a crack of possibility in a mountain of difficulties, the powerful drill that lets us tunnel through the solid rock of complacency and defeatism and move steadily ahead toward triumph. A mindset of invincibility is your most powerful inner tool for transforming any event or circumstance into inner wisdom and soul growth. Invincible thinking will give you all the nourishment you'll ever need to fulfill your purpose in life and become a guiding light for others.

THE LAWS OF SUCCESS
A Spiritual Guide to Turning Your Hopes Into Reality

Softcover | 208 pages | $15.95 | ISBN: 978-1-942125-15-0

The Laws of Success offers 8 spiritual principles that, when put to practice in our day-to-day life, will help us attain lasting success and let us experience the fulfillment of living our purpose and the joy of sharing our happiness with many others. The timeless wisdom and practical steps that Okawa offers will guide us through any difficulties and problems we may face in life, and serve as guiding principles for living a positive, constructive, and meaningful life.

THE LAWS OF INVINCIBLE LEADERSHIP
An Empowering Guide for Continuous and Lasting Success in
Business and in Life

Hardcover | 224 pages | $19.95 | ISBN: 978-1- 942125-30- 3

Ryuho Okawa shares essential principles for all who wish to become invincible managers and leaders in their fields of work, organizations, societies, and nations. Let Okawa's breakthrough management philosophy in this empowering guide help you find the seeds of your future success. Your Keys to becoming an invincible overall winner in life and in business are just pages away.

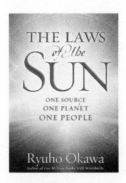

THE LAWS OF THE SUN
One Source, One Planet, One People

Hardcover | 264 pages | $24.95 | ISBN: 978-1-937673-04-8

Imagine if you could ask God why he created this world and what spiritual laws he used to shape us—and everything around us. In *The Laws of the Sun*, Okawa outlines these laws of the universe and provides a road map for living one's life with greater purpose and meaning. This powerful book shows the way to realize true happiness—a happiness that continues from this world through the other.

A LIFE OF TRIUMPH
Unleashing Your Light Upon the World

Softcover | 240 pages | $15.95 | ISBN: 978-1-942125-11-2

There is a power within you that can lift your heart from despair to hope, from hardship to happiness, and from defeat to triumph. In this book, Ryuho Okawa explains the key attitudes that will help you continuously tap the everlasting reserves of positivity, courage, and energy that are already a part of you so you can realize your dreams and become a wellspring of happiness. You'll also find many inspirational poems and a contemplation exercise to inspire your inner light in times of adversity and in your day-to-day life.

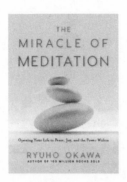

THE MIRACLE OF MEDITATION
Opening Your Life to Peace, Joy, and the Power Within

Softcover | 208 pages | $15.95 | ISBN: 978-1-942125-09-9

Meditation can open your mind to the self-transformative potential within and connect your soul to the wisdom of heaven—all through the power of belief. This book combines the power of faith and the practice of meditation to help you create inner peace, discover your inner divinity, become your ideal self, and cultivate a purposeful life of altruism and compassion.

THE LAWS OF FAITH
One World Beyond Differences

THE LAWS OF MISSION
Essential Truths for Spiritual Awakening in a Secular Age

HEALING FROM WITHIN
Life-Changing Keys to Calm, Spiritual, and Healthy Living

THE UNHAPPINESS SYNDROME
28 Habits of Unhappy People (and How to Change Them)

THE ESSENCE OF BUDDHA
The Path to Enlightenment

THE LAWS OF JUSTICE
How We Can Solve World Conflicts and Bring Peace

THE HEART OF WORK
10 Keys to Living Your Calling

THINK BIG!
Be Positive and Be Brave to Achieve Your Dreams

INVITATION TO HAPPINESS
7 Inspirations from Your Inner Angel

MESSAGES FROM HEAVEN
What Jesus, Buddha, Muhammad, and Moses Would Say Today

SECRETS OF THE EVERLASTING TRUTHS
A New Paradigm for Living on Earth

THE NINE DIMENSIONS
Unveiling the Laws of Eternity

THE MOMENT OF TRUTH
Become a Living Angel Today

CHANGE YOUR LIFE, CHANGE THE WORLD
A Spiritual Guide to Living Now

For a complete list of books, visit OkawaBooks.com